D0822546
MONTHLY
GIRLS'
NOZAKI
-KUN
13
Izumi Tsubaki

MONTHLY GIRLS' NOZAKI-KUN 13

contents

Issue 119 : 003

Issue 120 : 017

Issue 121 : 035

Issue 122 : 059

Issue 123 : 077

Issue 124 : 095

Issue 125 : 111

Issue 126 : 129

Issue 127 : 147

Issue 128 : 161

[ISSUE 119]

LEAVE IT TO ME!

OH, BY THE WAY ...
...I'M NOT GONNA HAVE MUCH FREE TIME BEFORE YOUR NEXT DEADLINE.
I'VE GOT SOME STUFF COMING UP.
WHAA!?
REALLY!?

...IT SEEMS LIKE THE BACKGROUND PERSON CAN ONLY MAKE IT FOR ABOUT HALF OF THE USUAL AMOUNT OF TIME.
...SO ...
HUH!? ARE YOU GONNA BE ALL RIGHT!?
I'LL MAKE IT WORK.

I MAY NOT LOOK THE PART, BUT...
...I AM A PRO.
!!
NOZAKI ...!!

I just gotta come up with a draft that doesn't need as many backgrounds ...!
I'M SURE I CAN PULL IT OFF IF I TRY!!
NOZAKI ...!!!

DESPERATE MEASURES

WAIT...BUT DIDN'T LAST CHAPTER END WITH THEM ALL GOING, "*Now it's time for a party to celebrate!!*"?
OKAY, CHEERS!
TO BE CONTINUED
NEXT TIME, A PARTY! ♡
LET'S CANCEL IT.
THAT'S A JOKE, RIGHT!!?

OKAY... THEN HOW ABOUT THIS?
THEY HAVE THE PARTY, BUT...
...SUZUKI AND MAMIKO AREN'T ALLOWED TO BE THERE.
NO WAY!
YOU'RE ALWAYS SO MEAN TO YOUR MAIN CHARACTERS!!!

BUT IF THE PROTAGS CAN'T GO...
...WHY EVEN HAVE A PARTY!!?
THERE'S NO POINT TO THAT!!!
HEH...
THINK ABOUT IT, MIKOSHIBA.
IF THE MAIN CHARACTERS AREN'T ACTUALLY THERE, IT'LL...

① FOOD
Huh?
② BACKGROUND
③ CUPS
Where are Mamiko and Suzuki-kun?
...BE OVER IN THREE PANELS!!!
DUDE...! YOU ADD TONS OF POINTLESS SIDE STORIES ALL THE TIME...!!!
IT'S COMPLETELY NECESSARY.
THIS IS ESSENTIAL!

UNTIL THE PARTY ENDS

OKAY... SINCE BACK-GROUNDS ARE A NO-GO...
THEN IT'D FEEL LIKE A PARTY, EVEN WITHOUT ALL SORTS OF BACKGROUNDS.
...CAN'T YOU AT LEAST MAKE IT WORK BY DRAWING FOOD?
HMM... IF I'M THE ONE DOING IT, THEN THE MENU AT THE PARTY...

...WILL BE JUST WATER BOTTLES AND SQUARE SNACKS...
CAN DRAW
CAN DRAW
CAN DRAW
CAN DRAW
CAN DRAW
CAN DRAW
CAN MUDDLE THROUGH IT
ビスケット
WHEN DID IT TURN INTO A FIELD TRIP ...!!!?

BOX: BISCUITS

OKAY, SURE! THEY ARE IN HIGH SCHOOL, AFTER ALL!
CAN'T YOU GO WITH THAT!? SNACKS AND WATER BOTTLES !!
AS LONG AS THEY'RE EATING AND HAVING FUN!!
...BY THE WAY...
...THESE WATER BOTTLES AND SNACK BOXES...

...DON'T OPEN. THEY CAN NEVER OPEN.
CAN'T DRAW THIS PART
CAN'T DRAW WHAT'S INSIDE
Box
ビスケット
HE'D ONLY BE HOLDING THEM.
WHY'S THIS GUY TRYIN' TO SHOW ME HIS BISCUITS?

THE REAL ANSWER

FINE.
WE'LL FINISH THE PARTY IN THREE PANELS.
THERE'S NO OTHER CHOICE.
BUT THEN...
...WHERE ARE MAMIKO AND SUZUKI GONNA BE DURING THAT TIME?
HMM... LET'S SEE...
IT'D BE MOST NATURAL IF THEY WERE LOCKED UP.
MAYBE KIDNAPPED?

SUZUKI-KUN...
...I THINK...
...WE'RE TRAPPED IN HERE...
NO WAY...
WHY WOULD SOMEONE DO THIS TO US...?
'COS IT'S EASIER ON YOUR CREATOR...

A CLASSROOM...
...HAS TOO MANY DESKS. THAT'S HARD.
SO JUST AS THEY WERE PUTTING AWAY GYM EQUIPMENT...
...THEY FOUND THEMSELVES TRAPPED IN ONE OF THE GYM STORAGE ROOMS—WITH NOT A THING IN SIGHT...

OH NO...
THERE'S NOTHING HERE TO HELP US ESCAPE...
A STORAGE ROOM WHILE WE WERE TIDYING UP...
D'YOU THINK SOMEONE DID THIS TO US ON PURPOSE...!?
BUT WHO COULD IT BE...!!?
YOUR CREATOR...

THE POWER OF WARM FUZZIES

SO WHAT ARE YOU GONNA DO...?
WILL THEY BE STUCK IN HERE THE WHOLE TIME...?
NAH.
THEY'LL GET OUT RIGHT AT THE END.
OH!
YEAH, THEY CAN'T BE IN TOTAL DARKNESS THE ENTIRE CHAPTER!
GOOD ONE!

WE FINALLY...
...GOT OUT.
LOOK.
IT'S ALREADY...
...DARK OUT...
SO IT'S DARK OUTSIDE TOO!!?

HUH?
WAIT A MINUTE. WHERE ARE THEY RIGHT NOW ANYWAY?
WHERE ARE THE GYM STORAGE ROOMS AGAIN?
......
WE SHOULD GET BACK TO CLASS.
KYU (SQUEEZE)
きゅ
SUZUKI-KUN.
MAMI-KO?
I...
...WAS SO SCARED.

BUT WHEN I'M WITH YOU...
...I FEEL LIKE I CAN DO ANY-THING.
I WONDER WHY...
HEY! SERIOUSLY, WHERE ARE THEY RIGHT NOW!?
DAM-MIT!!!
DON'T MAKE IT ALL WARM AND FUZZY!!!

A PLACE WE CAN CREATE

HMM...? WAIT...
I CAN DRAW GRASS AND TREES.
I LIKE NATURE.
OHHH!!!
SO WHAT'S THAT MEAN!?

I COULD DO A PLACE LIKE THIS.
RIGHT BEHIND THE STORAGE ROOMS...
...THERE WAS A PLACE LIKE THIS...?
...I HAD NO IDEA...
ざぁ… ZAA (WHOOSH)
NEITHER DID I!

BUT YOU KNOW... ...IT'S MISSING A CERTAIN SOME-THING.
THERE'S JUST TREES AND GRASS...
UH...
I DON'T THINK THAT'S THE ISSUE...
I'VE GOT IT!
YOU SHOULD ADD SOME FLOWERS, MIKOSHIBA...
WHA!?
THERE!!! HOW'S THAT!?

PLACE THEY'VE NEVER LAID EYES ON BEFORE
OUT-OF-PLACE FIELD OF FLOWERS
THE AFTER-LIFE...

YOU'RE THOSE TWO...!

IS THIS HOW THIS CHAPTER ENDS, THEN?
WITH NO IDEA WHO DID IT?
NO. AS A PRO, I CAN'T LEAVE IT HANGING LIKE THAT.
AND AS A PRO, I SHOULD PROBABLY FORE-SHADOW IT A BIT.
?
FORE-SHADOW ...?

THE PERSON WHO TRAPPED THEM IN THAT ROOM WAS A GIRL FROM THEIR CLASS.
MAMI-KO! YOU...
...JUST HAD TO GO AFTER MY BELOVED KIMURA-KUN, DIDN'T YOU?
THAT GIRL ...!!!
SHE WAS HOLDING THE SQUARE SNACKS AT THE PARTY EARLIER ...!!!

BUT IT WAS ALL ONE BIG MIX-UP—
AOTA ...
WHAT DID YOU DO...?
KI-MURA-KUN!!?
YOU'RE THE ONLY ONE...
...FOR ME, AOTA !!!
THE BOY WITH THE SQUARE SNACKS !!!

BOX: BISCUITS

I'M SO SORRY...
IT'S ALL RIGHT.
WE CAN HAVE...
...OUR OWN PARTY!
WE'RE GOOD!
...AT LEAST TAKE THESE.
THEN ...
FOR YOU...
ビスケット
THE SQUARE SNACKS !!!

SHE READS WITH HER FEELINGS

I DON'T FEEL RIGHT ABOUT THIS...
LET'S ASK SOMEONE ELSE TO TAKE A LOOK.
OH!
HEY, SAKURA!
C'MERE!!!
READ THIS!!

......
MOKU (ABSORBED)
MOKU
PIRA (FLIP)
YOU GOTTA SEE IT TOO—
HOW STRANGE THESE ITEMS AND BACK-GROUNDS ARE...!!!

THAT SCENE IN THE FLOWER FIELD AT THE END WAS SO PRETTY! ♡
TEE HEE HEE!
IT REALLY GRABS YOUR ATTENTION!
ARE YOU KIDDING ME!!!?
THAT WAS THE WEIRDEST PART!!!

OH... AND THOSE BISCUITS LOOKED REALLY GOOD.
YOU GOTTA BE KIDDING ME!!!

FALLEN PAGES

HUH!?
THAT'S A JOKE, RIGHT?
YOU NEVER SEE WHAT'S IN THE BOX?
BUT THEY'RE BISCUITS!
......
HOLD ON!
WHY HASN'T HE EVEN OPENED THEM!?
HE'S JUST HOLDING THEM!!
BASA (RUSTLE)
ばさっ
BASA
ばさ

......
HORI-SENPAI!!?

AAAH!
THAT'S PART OF NOZAKI'S ROUGH DRAFT ...!!!
DID WE DROP IT!!?
OH NOOO ...!!!
HE'S GONNA SEE IT ...!!!
WHICH PAGE IS HE READING RIGHT NOW...!!?
BUT WHAT PART!?

HUH ......?
THEY DIED...?
OH.
THE FLOWER-FIELD SCENE !!!

HIS THOUGHTS ON THE MANGA

WAIT... SO NOW HORI-SENPAI KNOWS. YOU COOL WITH THAT, NOZAKI!!?
......
HE LOOKS SUPER-CONFUSED...
HE'S PROLLY NOT USED TO READING SHOUJO MANGA...

HUH—!?
HE PULLED OUT HIS OWN NOTEBOOK!?
NO WAY.
IS HE WRITING DOWN A REVIEW OR WHAT!!?

ZAKA (SKRITCH)
B
School Building A
Courtyard
ZAKA
Gym
Cafeteria
THAT'S...
...A SKETCH OF MAMIKO'S SCHOOL...!!?

URO (WAVER)
Gym
Storage Room
?
URO
Field of Flowers?
THAT FIELD OF FLOWERS DOESN'T MAKE ANY KIND OF SENSE, DOES IT!!?

INVISIBLE ONLY TO ME

THE LOCATION OF THAT FLOWER FIELD IS REALLY WEIRD, ISN'T IT!!?
ISN'T IT!!?
Y-YEAH.
SO YOU READ IT TOO, MIKO-SHIBA?
THIS THING?

I TOTALLY DID!!
AND WHAT'S MORE...
HAH!
WAIT, NO ...!!!
I GOTTA TALK ABOUT IT LIKE I'M A COMMON READER ...!!!
※ HORI DOESN'T KNOW YET.

TH—
THAT SCENE IN THE FLOWER FIELD AT THE END WAS SO PRETTY! ♡
HUH.
YEAH ...
OKAY...
OH... AND THOSE BISCUITS LOOKED REALLY GOOD. ♡

BISCUITS? OH...
YOU MEAN THE ONES THEIR CLASSMATES WERE EATING.
YEAH, THOSE.
YOU'RE JOKING, RIGHT!!?

BETTER LEFT UNSAID

OH! NOZAKI-KUN!!!
MIKORIN AND HORI-SENPAI ARE TALKING ABOUT MANGA!!
OHH ...!
MY BACKGROUND GUY AND MY FLOWER GUY ARE TALKING SHOP WITHOUT REALIZING IT...!!

MIKOSHIBA ALWAYS GUSHES OVER HORI-SENPAI'S BACKGROUNDS.
WOW!
THIS IS GREAT!
I BET HE'D BE REALLY SURPRISED TO LEARN HORI-SENPAI DOES THEM!
OH-HO-HO-HO-HO-HO-HO-HO!

SERIOUSLY, THEY AREN'T EATING ANY BISCUITS!!!
DID YOU EVEN PAY ATTEN-TION!?
AND THIS BACK-GROUND!!
LOOK! DOES IT MAKE ANY SENSE TO YOU!!?

WAIT... IT'S NOT LIKE YOU'D KNOW ANYTHING ABOUT BACK-GROUNDS ANYWAY!!!
AAAARGH! NO ONE GETS IT!!
OOOOOF.

PUSHING THE WORK OFF ON SOMEONE ELSE

Y'KNOW, I SAW YOUR DRAFT AT SCHOOL.
I TOLD YOU, "I DON'T HAVE A LOT OF TIME, SO I'LL WORK FASTER TO MAKE IT UP."
I NEVER SAID YOU SHOULD CUT DOWN ON BACK-GROUNDS...
HUH!!?
THAT'S WHAT YOU SAID!!?

SO HOW MUCH DID YOU CUT IT DOWN TO ANYWAY?
ONE.
TWO.
THREE ...

EIGHT !!?
THIRTY PAGES—BUT ONLY EIGHT BACKGROUND PANELS!!?
YOU'RE KIDDING, RIGHT!?
AH HA HA HA.
THAT'S PRETTY IMPRES-SIVE!
SO I'LL NEED TONE IN PRETTY MUCH ALL OF THE PANELS THIS TIME INSTEAD.
AH HA HA HA HA HA!
ALL OF THE PANELS?

......
HUH?
IN CHARGE OF SCREEN TONE

[ISSUE 120]

BEGINNER MISTAKES

YOU'VE GOTTEN WAY BETTER AT APPLYING TONE LATELY, WAKAMATSU.
LOOKING GOOD!
HEE HEE HEE!
YOU THINK SO?

SERIOUSLY! THIS PART WHERE YOU BLUR IT OUT LIKE THAT IS PRETTY HARD, RIGHT?
SO, UHHH, YOU TAKE YOUR BLADE AND THEN...
...SCRAPE DIAGONALLY, LIKE THIS. IT TOOK A WHILE TO GET USED TO...

...but! Now I can even do a perfect tone flash, no problem!!!
DON (THUMP)
I don't screw up anything while using tone these days! Not one bit!!
BWA HA HA HA!!!

......
THERE'S SOME SORT OF STICKER STUCK TO HIS BACK.
WONDER WHAT IT IS...

RECOVERED OBJECTS

...SO ANYWAY...
...I NOTICED STRANGE STICKERS THAT WERE STUCK TO YOUNG WAKAMATSU'S BACK.
I WONDER WHAT THEY COULD BE...
TH—
THOSE THINGS ...!!!

ARE THEY THE SAME AS THE ONES I SOMETIMES SEE ON MIYAKO'S CLOTHES ...!!?
MORNING.
THOSE
THINGS

SO...
...THIS IS THE STICKER THAT I TOOK OFF HIM...
LET'S TRY PUTTING IT ON A PIECE OF WHITE PAPER.
PETA (PLOP)
OH, HEY !!!
YEAH, THAT'S IT! LOOKS LIKE...SOME KINDA POLKA-DOT PATTERN !!?
YEAH, THAT!!!
AND THEN THIS ONE.
PETA
OHH !!
I'VE SEEN THAT ONE TOO...
PETA
AND THIS.
AND THIS ONE.
HUH ...?
WHAT'S THAT S'POSED TO BE ...?
PETA
WAIT!
DID WAKAMATSU-KUN REALLY HAVE ALL OF THESE ON HIM?
ISN'T THAT A BIT MUCH?

ASKING AROUND

WHAT ARE THESE ANYWAY? SOME ARE EVEN GRADIENT ONES.
ESS-EEE 30?
HMMM.
I'LL GO ASK AROUND.

HELLO, LADIES.
WOULD YOU MIND IF I ASKED YOU A QUICK QUESTION ...?
WHAT IS IT, KASHIMA-KUN? ♡
YOU CAN ASK ME ANY-THING!
IT'S ABOUT THESE STICKERS.

HAVE ANY OF YOU SEEN THEM BEFORE?

WHAT ARE THOSE ...?
EEP!
I DON'T KNOW!
EEP!
TWO OF THEM ARE ACTING REALLY WEIRD.

COMRADES

SEE, I FOUND THESE STUCK TO A FRIEND'S CLOTHES.
WHA? REALLY!!?
WONDER IF HIS GIRLFRIEND WAS PLAYING A PRANK ON HIM!
THAT'S SO CUTE! ♡

THEY LOOK LIKE THEY WANNA YELL AT THEM...
AND THEIR FACES ARE LIKE... "WHOA, HE MESSED UP"...!!

HE'S HAD THEM ON HIM PRETTY MUCH EVERY DAY LATELY...
...THESE STICKERS.
HUH? EVERY DAY?
I CAN'T IMAGINE WHY!
I DON'T GET IIIT!

NOW THEY'RE LIKE, "HANG IN THERE" ...!!
AND "DON'T PUSH YOURSELF TOO HARD" ...!!!

FAMILIAR FOREIGN OBJECTS

OH?
RYOUSUKE-KUN... AND THAT GIRL WHO WORKS HERE...?
THEY'RE PORING OVER A PIECE OF PAPER. MAYBE HE'S HELPING HER WITH SOME HOMEWORK...
ほのぼの…
HONOBONO (TOUCHED)

OH, MIYAKO. PERFECT TIMING.
WHAT'S WITH THESE STICKERS...?
WE ASKED SOME GIRLS ABOUT THEM...
...BUT ALL THEY SAID WAS, "YOU'RE BETTER OFF NOT KNOWING"...

WELL...
...YOU TWO ARE INNOCENTS. YOU AREN'T INVOLVED IN THIS...
...SO YOU'RE BETTER OFF NOT KNOWING...
IS THIS A HORROR STORY!!? IT REALLY IS A HORROR STORY, ISN'T IT!!?
MIYA-KOOO!!!

IF YOU DON'T SAY ANYTHING...

A HORROR STORY...
THEN THESE STICKERS...
YEAH... THEY...
...DRAIN THE LIFE FORCE OF ANY HUMAN THEY'RE STUCK TO.
YORO よろ
YORO (STAGGER) よろ
GESSORI (SLUMP) げっそり
THEY'RE CURSED ...!!!
KA (FLASH) カッ

THAT'S NOT IT AT ALL...
...BUT IF I PUSH BACK, I'LL HAVE TO ANSWER THEIR QUESTIONS...
I'LL JUST LET IT SLIDE ...

MIYAKO, THAT'S IT, ISN'T IT!!?
......
SU (FWISH)
SHE'S NOT DENYING IT...!?
SO THAT IS IT!!! YOU DID SAY YOUR HAIR WASN'T DOING SO GREAT LATELY, AFTER ALL!!!

NO WAY... BUT IT'S REALLY PRETTY!!!
NOPE! HER HAIR IS USUALLY WAY SMOOTHER AND SHINIER!!
BUT IT ALREADY SEEMS LIKE SILK TO ME.
ARE YOU BLIND? HER HAIR IS, WELL...
STOP IT!!!

SKILLED AT CUTTING

SORRY ABOUT THIS, WAKA-MATSU.
I ASKED FOR WAY TOO MUCH TONE THIS TIME...
AH HA HA!
IT'S OKAY.

ACTUALLY, SINCE THERE'S SO MUCH TONE IN THE BACKGROUNDS THIS TIME, THERE ARE A LOT OF INTERESTING SCRAPS LEFT OVER.
THERE!
PERI (PEEL)
HEH HEH HEH!
I GOT IT OFF IN ONE PIECE!
HEE HEE HEE HEE!

SEN-PAAAI !!!
GASHI (CLUTCH)
WHAT !!?
A-A BLACK SHADOW...!!! A POSSESSED TALISMAN...!!! STUCK RIGHT TO HIS BACK ...!!!
IT'S WAY TOO EARLY FOR GHOST STORIES !!!

UNREST

ON WAKA-MATSU'S BACK?
HUH...?
SOMETHING STUCK TO...

...HIS BACK ...?

HEEEEY, WAKA-MATSU !!!
PERI
べリッ
GOOD LUCK WITH CLASS!
しゅたっ
SHUTA (FWOOSH)
TOO CLOSE ...
OH YEAH... HE'S BEEN DOING A LOT OF TONE WORK LATELY.
きゅ
KYU (GRAB)

HUH ...?
WHAT ...?
...I'LL BE RIGHT THERE WITH YOU WHEN YOU FALL TO THE CURSE...
GYU (SQUEEZE)
ぎゅっ
WHAT WH— THE!!?

SHE'S STRONG

YOUNG WAKAMATSU SURE DOES SEEM WORN OUT TODAY...
HE'S GONNA BE IN TROUBLE AT THIS RATE...
HAH!
THERE'S A STICKER ON CHIYO-CHAN'S BACK...!!!

SA-KURA.
THERE'S SOME-THING STUCK TO YOU.
SU (BRUSH)
HUH!?
OH YEAH!!!
THANKS!!!

WHAT'S GOING ON...?
THIS CURSE HAS YOUNG WAKA-MATSU IN SHAMBLES, BUT CHIYO-CHAN...
...BRUSHED IT OFF LIKE IT WAS NOTHING ...?

PETA (STICK)
CHIYO-CHAN!!?

THE CONCLUSION SHE'S BEEN LED TO

SORRY.
THERE'S ONE HERE TOO.
PERI (PEEL)
I'M NOT ONLY MAKING THINGS ROUGH FOR WAKAMATSU, BUT YOU TOO...
NOZAKI'S THE ONE BEHIND THIS...!!?
!

I SEE...SO A CURSE PLACED ON NOZAKI TRANS-FERRED TO THEM...?
COME TO THINK OF IT, HE DOES LOOK KINDA...
...WELL, I CAN'T REALLY TELL WITH HIM...

NO. NEVER MIND THAT. THINK OF CHIYO-CHAN...
FOR SUCH A SMALL GIRL TO HAVE HER LIFE FORCE DRAINED BY A CURSE...
SHE LOOKS REALLY HEALTHY, THOUGH.

MAYBE THE PROBLEM IS YOUR MENTAL FORTITUDE ...?
NEVER FEAR.
IF YOU HARDEN YOUR HEART, THAT CURSE WILL BE NO MATCH FOR YOU.
HUH ...!?
WHAT'S GOTTEN INTO YOU...!!?
C— CURSE !!?

A TERRIFYING KOUHAI

I'M DOING IT AS WELL, BUT I'M DEFINITELY PUTTING TOO MUCH ON WAKAMATSU...
ALL RIGHT. I SHOULD AT LEAST GIVE HIM TODAY OFF...
UHHH...
O—

OH HO HO HO!
HOW UNCOUTH, CINDERELLA!!!
GET DOWN ON YOUR KNEES AND BEG FOR FORGIVENESS!!!

HEY! I CAN SEE HOW EMBARRASSED YOU ARE!!! PUT SOME HEART INTO IT!!!
FOCUS, FOCUS!!!
FOCUS, FOCUS!!!
HECKLING

SHE SAID SOMETHING ABOUT MENTAL-FORTITUDE TRAINING FOR WAKAMATSU.
SHE'S ACTUALLY PUTTING EFFORT INTO SOMETHING FOR ONCE.
PUTTING MENTAL PRESSURE ON HIMSELF WHEN HE'S ALREADY PHYSICALLY EXHAUSTED...?
ZO (SHUDDER)
IS HE A MASOCHIST OR WHAT ...!?

THIS IS THE PROBLEM WITH HER!

HOW DID I END UP LIKE THIS...?

I JUST HAPPENED TO BE HERE...

I DUNNO ...

HMM?

WHAT'S THIS?

PERI (PEEL)

......
AAAAAH!
....

A FEW DAYS LATER
PERI
......
PERI
PERI
I DON'T KNOW WHY...
...BUT SHE'S TAKING THE TONE OFF OF ME WITHOUT SAYING A WORD...
IS THIS ...
...HER WAY OF ROOTING FOR ME...?

AFTER THE DEAD-LINE
WHERE ARE THEY!!?
WHAA!? I CAN'T FIND ANY STICKERS !!!
IT WAS JUST FUN FOR HER TO PULL THEM OFF OF ME!!!

A MAN WHO DEFIES EXPECTATIONS

SO...
...YOUNG WAKAMATSU OVERCAME HIS CURSE.
HIS BACK IS TOTALLY CLEAR NOW.
PHEW...
GOOD FOR WAKAMATSU-KUN!!!
SO THEY REALLY DID STICK WITH THE CURSE THING...

OH WELL... I GUESS IF RYOUSUKE-KUN IS SCARED, IT WORKS OUT FOR ME...
HE'D PROLLY RUN AWAY IF HE SAW ANY TONE ON ME...
OH!
MIYAKO!

PERI (PEEL)
GUSHA (CRUMPLE)
...UHH.
YOU HAD SOMETHING ON YOU...

....
TH—
THANKS...

SHE... ...REACTED TO THAT SCREEN TONE EARLIER...
KASHIMA-KUN WAS SO COOL TODAY!
I KNOW, RIGHT?
SINCE SHE REACTED TO TONE LIKE THAT...
...SHE MUST BE IN PRETTY DEEP...
I CAN'T BELIEVE SHE TALKED TO US!

THEY WERE TOTALLY FEELING EACH OTHER OUT ON THE WAY HOME.

[Extra]

IT HAPPENS ALL THE TIME

POLKA-DOT STICKERS ...?

SO WHAT ...

...ARE THESE STICKERS ANYWAY?

THAT ONE'S CALLED #62.

AND THAT'S #64.

HUH ...?
SO THEY'RE NAMED IN ORDER OF HOW DARK THEY ARE...?
THEY'RE GETTING DARKER...
62
63
64
40
42
45
PETA (STICK)

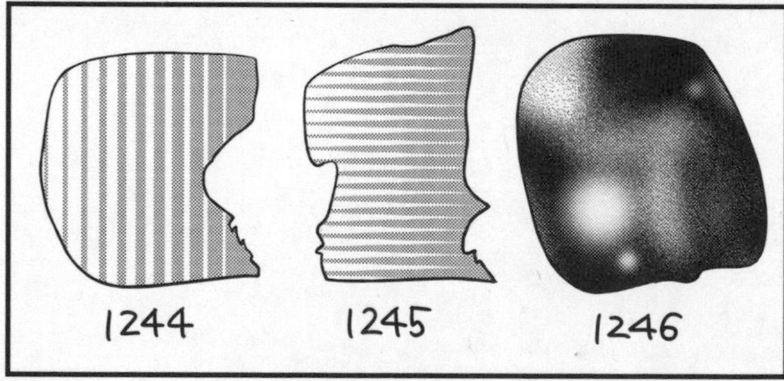
1244
1245
1246

WHAT HAPPENED BETWEEN 1245 AND 1246...!!?

[Extra]

A CURIOUS TRUTH

SENPAI... DO YOU THINK YOUNG WAKAMATSU MIGHT'VE HAD MULTIPLE CURSES ON HIM...?
......
WHY D'YOU SAY THAT...?

FIRST, TAKE A LOOK AT THIS...
IT'S IN THE SHAPE OF A PERSON...SO IT MUST BE SOME SORT OF CURSED EFFIGY.
THAT'S A CUT-OUT OF SUZUKI...

AND THEN THERE WAS THIS ONE WITH DARK SPLOTCHES, LIKE BLOOD SPATTER...
I FEEL INTENSE HATRED FROM THIS ONE.
THAT'S A MAMIKO-FEELS-SHOCKED TONE...

AND HERE'S THE THIRD ONE.
THIS...IS THE CURSE OF A BABY CHICK THAT NEVER HATCHED...
HUH...? WHAT IS THAT? WHERE'D HE USE THIS ONE...?

MONTHLY GIRLS' × NOZAKI-KUN

[ISSUE 121]

HIDDEN TREASURES OF A HIGH SCHOOL BOY

THIS MIGHT BE A BIT OFF-TOPIC...

...BUT THERE'S A ROOM AT NOZAKI'S PLACE WHERE ENTRY IS BANNED.

DON'T OPEN THAT DOOR.

IS IT SOME KINDA STORAGE CLOSET...?

WHAT COULD HE...

...BE HIDING IN THERE...?

THE TYPE OF STUFF A BOY HIS AGE WOULD HIDE IS...
BUT WAIT... THIS IS NOZAKI WE'RE TALKING ABOUT...
IT'S PROLLY JUST WEIRD COS-TUMES.
FOR SUZUKI
FOR MAMIKO
OR...
...MAYBE IT'S A HUGE INSTRU-MENT...

BOOKS: SEXY x CUTE, BOUNCY HEAVEN, E-CUP ANGEL

セクシー×カワイ
ボヨヨン天国
Eカップ エンジェ
HUH...? MANGA...?
WHAT ARE THESE DOING IN HERE...? U-UHH...
OHHHH—!!! THEY'RE PORN—!!!
IT WAS TOO NOR-MAL, SO IT TOOK HIM A WHILE TO GET IT.

A NATURAL EXCUSE

OH, SENPAI.
DID YOU FIND A NEW RULER?
I'M PRETTY SURE I HAVE SOME SPARES IN THE BACK ROOM...
NOZAKI ...

DO YOU...
...READ THAT MANGA ...?
!!!
HAH!
CRAP ...!!!
MIKO-SHIBA'S COLLEC-TION ...!!!

I GOTTA THROW HIM OFF THE SCENT...!!!
DON'T YOU DARE TELL HIM IT'S MINE!!
U— UHHH ...
YEAH ...
ACTUALLY, I DO READ THOSE IN SECRET...

?
WHY DOES...
...HE LOOK SO UTTERLY BAFFLED ...!!?

THE ANSWER HE WAS LED TO

HUH...? YOU READ THAT KINDA STUFF ...?
FOR REAL?
I— I REALLY DO!!
YOU DON'T ... ...HAVE THEM 'COS "THE SPINES ARE CUTE ♡" ...?
ALL PINK AND COLORFUL...
I ACTUALLY READ THEM!!
OBVIOUSLY!!!

THEN WHAT'S THIS STORY ABOUT ...?
どっちが
いいの?
T—
TWO GIRLS FIGHTING FOR A CHANCE TO BE A SWIMWEAR MODEL!!!

BOOK: WHICH ONE?

WHAT ABOUT THIS ONE?
わがまま
Body☆Girl
TH—
THE SPOILED HEROINE MEETS THE PROTAGONIST AND LEARNS HOW TO CHANGE!!!

BOOK: SELFISH BODY ☆ GIRL

Happening Scramble
A—
A HAPPY ...
...SC... SCR... SCRUM! HOW TO FORM ONE!!!
YOU'RE NOT VERY GOOD AT ENGLISH, ARE YOU?
THAT SAYS "HAPPENING SCRAMBLE."

IT WAS DISCUSSED BEFOREHAND

THOSE CLEARLY AREN'T NOZAKI'S ...

...SO...

... THOSE TWO ...?

NOPE.

NOT THEM ...

THEY AREN'T YOURS, ARE THEY...
... YOUNGER NOZAKI?

......
LISTEN UP!!
DON'T YOU DARE TELL ANYONE THEY'RE MINE, GOT IT!?
LET'S SEE...
JUST SAY ONE OF NOZAKI'S FRIENDS KEEPS THEM HERE.
HIS NAME IS TAKAHASHI... AND HE'S A FRIEND FROM JUNIOR HIGH.

THEY'RE ALL MINE.
DON (THUMP)
IT WAS TOO MUCH OF A PAIN.

HE JUST ADORES THEM

THIS FEELS FAKE...
THEY'RE REALLY YOURS ?
こくり
KOKURI (NOD)
I SEE...
SO THIS IS WHAT YOU'RE INTO...?

I LOVE IT.
ぎゅっ
GYU
ぎゅっ
GYU (HUG)
HIS WORDS AND ACTIONS TOTALLY FEEL FAKE!!!

I LOVE IT.
ぽん
PON (PAT)
ぽん
PON
WHY'D HE REPEAT IT!!?
AND YOU DON'T SLEEP WITH THEM!!!

すぅ…
SUU (ZZZ)
DON'T FALL ASLEEP!

AN IRREGULAR QUESTION

I DON'T THINK THEY'RE HIS...
...WHICH MEANS... THEY BELONG TO SOMEONE ELSE WHO'S OVER ALL THE TIME...
MIKO-SHIBA ...?
NOZAKI'S FRIEND

...MIKO-SHIBA...
ALL OF THOSE MANGA... JUST FOR HIM...?
AND...
...ALL OF THOSE NICHE GENRES FOR JUST ONE GUY...?
ZURARI (ORDERLY)
ずらり

I WONDER ...
HEY, MIKOSHIBA. SO THE MANGA THAT YOU'RE INTO...
PIKU (TWITCH)
ぴくっ
MANGA ...!!?
HA...
STAY COOL ...
YOU ALREADY HAVE A STORY READY FOR THIS EXACT SCENARIO.
"I READ THIS ONE SUPER-POPULAR SHOUNEN SERIES..."

WHAT COLOR ARE THE SPINES?
SP ...!?
SPINES ...!!?
WH-WHITE ...
RED ...!?
MAYBE BLUE ...!!!
? ? ?
? ? ?

THE MATCHING TITLE

SO THE TRUTH IS... I SAW THEM AT NOZAKI'S PLACE YESTERDAY.
SOME... MANGA...
HUH!!?
YOU DON'T MEAN ...?

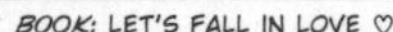
BOOK: LET'S FALL IN LOVE ♡

恋しよっ♡
DID HE FIGURE OUT THAT I'M THE FLOWER PERSON ...!!?
WHAT TYPE OF MANGA ...!?

ONES WITH A GIRL FRONT AND CENTER ON THE COVER...
THAT'S LET'S FALL IN LOVE ♡ !!!

BOOK: LET'S FALL IN LOVE ♡ BOOK: BOOBY ♡ BOUNTY

...WITH PINK SPINES...
...AND KINDA LOW-IQ TITLES...
おっぱい♡いっぱい
恋しよっ♡
THAT'S LET'S FALL IN LOVE ♡ FOR SURE!!!

JUDGING BASED ON APPEARANCES

WAIT, NO... IT'S NOT OVER YET. I CAN STILL GET OUT OF THIS...
...OH REALLY? YOU...
...THINK THAT'S ME...?
HUH?
CAN'T YOU THINK OF A MORE NATURAL FIT?

LIKE MAYBE SAKURA!!!
I DREW...
...A FLOWER!
SAKURA...!!?
HEH HEH HEH...
I REALLY WISH I HAD D CUPS.

I COULD MAYBE SEE IT IF YOU SAID KASHIMA'S SISTER, THOUGH...
NAH... NOT SA-KURA.
SO...
...LEWD!!
!!!
SA-KURA...!!!
...HE'S TOTALLY DISSING YOU...!!

BUT I GET IT!!!
I DREW IT.
I DREW SOME FLOWERS!

THEY'RE ON THE SAME PAGE?

BUT I STILL THINK YOU'RE THE MOST LIKELY CANDIDATE.
MORESO THAN SAKURA OR KASHIMA'S SISTER!
Y— YOU REALLY THINK SO!?

WELL... I GUESS I AM MORE ELEGANT...
AFTER ALL...
...I'M NOT ONLY DELICATE, BUT BOLD AND PUT TOGETHER— MUCH LIKE A SINGLE RED ROSE...

IS THAT WHAT YOU MEANT TO SAY ...?
HEH...
UH...
......
I... DON'T THINK WE'RE ON THE SAME PAGE...
MIKO-SHIBA ...

THAT'S RIGHT ...
YOU ARE AN EXQUISITE ROSE— SHINING MORE BEAUTIFULLY THAN ANY OTHER..
AND IN THE FACE OF SUCH LUSTER ...
...ON-LOOKERS CAN BUT SIT AND SIGH AT YOUR WONDER...
BUT HE'S ALL IN ANY-WAY.

PROFESSIONAL WILLPOWER

IT'S KINDA EMBARRASSING WHEN YOU PUT IT LIKE THAT!!
WELL, I GUESS I AM PRETTY GOOD AT DOING ROSES!!
HA-HA-HA-HA!
SHAKA (SKRITCH)
SHAKA
SHAKA

HERE.

BUT REALLY, I CAN'T BELIEVE YOU'RE NOT SURPRISED.
I'M A BIT SHOCKED THAT YOU FIGURED OUT I DRAW ALL THE FLOWERS, Y'KNOW.
HA-HA-HA-HA-HA.

...Beautiful things come from beautiful people...
That's only naaaaa... natural... after aaaaaa...
GACHI (FREEZE)
ガチッ
...SORRY. COULD WE TAKE IT FROM THE TOP?
ALL OUT OF WHACK

THE WORDS HE WAS HOLDING IN

DON'T TELL ANYONE ELSE, OKAY?

BYE!!!

ドゴッ
DOGO (THUD)
HUH?
SENPAI—!?
WHAT'S WRONG!?
...I—

ばっ
BA (FWOOSH)
FOR REAL!? NO WAY!
I HAD NO IDEA! WHAAA—!!?
A—
ABOUT WHAT!?

BUT I STILL DON'T KNOW WHOSE BOOKS THOSE ARE!!!
I CAN'T EXACTLY ASK NOW!!!
AT THIS POINT, GUESS I'LL JUST ASSUME THEY'RE YOUR SISTER'S!!!
WHAT THE HECK ARE YOU GOING ON ABOUT...!!?

WE HAVE AN UNDERSTANDING

OH, THAT'S RIGHT... MIKOSHIBA IS THE ONE WHO DOES THE FLOWERS...

I GUESS...

...HE DOES SPEND A LOT OF TIME HERE AT NOZAKI'S PLACE...

HMM. THAT MAKES SENSE.

NOW THAT I KNOW, IT MAKES LEAVING NOTES FOR HIM A LOT EASIER.
I'LL USE STICKY NOTES.
PETA (STICK)
Put some flowers here.
HMMM.
MAYBE I SHOULD THROW IN SOME SMALL TALK TOO.
NORMAL CHITCHAT LIKE...

I hear from Kashima that you have a test this week.
Go ahead and eat those snacks with Kashima.
Kashima has stuff
during lunch
Kashi

IS THE BACKGROUND PERSON STALKING KASHIMA OR, LIKE...?
THEY SUDDENLY SHOWED THEIR TRUE COLORS, HUH...?
HORI-SENPAI... ARE YOU TRYING TO GET FOUND OUT? YOU'RE BEING PRETTY OBVIOUS...

DON'T GET ANY CLOSER

MIKO-SHIBA.
THE BACK-GROUND PERSON LEFT THIS FOR YOU.
EEEK!!
THE BACK-GROUND PERSON ...!!
BIKU (JOLT)
WHAT'S WITH YOU?
?
WELL ...
...THE BACKGROUND PERSON ALWAYS FELT REALLY OUT OF REACH BEFORE, SO IT'S KINDA WEIRD THAT THEY'RE TRYING TO GET CLOSE TO ME OUTTA THE BLUE...
I MEAN, IF...
...SANTA WAS LIKE, "I'M OFF THIS SUNDAY. LET'S HANG OUT!" IT'S THAT GOT THAT TYPE OF AWKWARD VIBE...
EVEN IF YOU TRY TO GET CLOSER TO ME, IT'S JUST...
AN OFF-DUTY SANTA...?

[Extra]

HIS IDEAL DISTANCE

SO...
...YOU DON'T WANT ANY SMALL TALK?
AAA-ARGH...
NO, UH...IT'S MORE LIKE I WANT TO KEEP JUST THE RIGHT AMOUNT OF SPACE BETWEEN US...
?
HOW MUCH SPACE IS THAT?

MAYBE THE SORT OF DISTANCE YOU'D HAVE FROM SOMEONE YOU'VE SEEN ONLINE A COUPLE TIMES BEFORE...?
AS IN...
"OH, I'VE SEEN THAT PROFILE PIC BEFORE"...
HITOTOTO
THAT'S BASICALLY A COMPLETE STRANGER.

OKAY, FINE.
THEN SOMEONE YOU'VE TALKED TO ONLINE A COUPLE OF TIMES...
I SEE. SO YOU DON'T WANNA TALK TO THEM IN REAL LIFE, BUT ONLINE IT'S ALL RIGHT.
YEAH, RIGHT.

LIKE THIS CHAT...?
TAKASHI
@ takashi-mote2 xxx
I asked a girl I like out on a date, and she said, "I like you, but getting together with you on the weekends is just too much."
Yuuji @
I'm crying
MIKO10 @
I'm crying
Ringo @
I'm crying
Asahi @
No way she likes you
CAN'T THEY BE D.M.ING ME?

[Extra]

AN OBSCURED VIEW

SA-KURA ...

...D'YOU KNOW WHO DOES THE BACK-GROUNDS?

YEAH!!

I DO!!

WH—
WHAT ARE THEY LIKE...?
UM, WELL ...
OH !!!
DON'T SAY ANYTHING SPECIFIC!!! TRY TO OBSCURE IT A LITTLE!!!
GOT IT!!
UMM...

BOYAAA (BLURRY)
ぼやぁ〜〜
......
BLUE.

SU (FWISH)
すっ…
HUH ......!!?
THAT'S IT!!!?

[Extra]

VAGUE DETAILS

A LITTLE MORE!!!
JUST GIMME A LITTLE BIGGER HINT!!!
JUST A LITTLE!!!
WHAA?
YOU'RE REALLY INTERESTED IN THEM, AREN'T YOU, MIKO-RIN?
HMM, LET'S SEE.
WELL...

STRAW-LIKE HAIR...
...I GUESS.
LIKE, A STRAW COLOR!!?
OR IT FEELS LIKE STRAW!!?
WHICH ONE!!?

SMALL.
WHAT IS!!?

DROOPY.
DROOPY WHERE!!?

[Extra]

TELL ME MORE

YOU'RE AMAZING, SAKURA.
YOU HAVE MIKOSHIBA TOTALLY HOOKED...
ANSWERS
STRAW-COLORED HAIR
DROOPY EYES
SMALL
SOWA (FIDGET)
SOWA
SOWA

O-OKAY.
HOW 'BOUT THIS, SAKURA!!?
WHAT D'YOU THINK OF THEM!?
TELL ME!!!
HUH? ME?
HMMM, LET'S SEE...

SERIOUS!!
THEY'RE VERY GOOD AT DRAWING BACKGROUNDS AND ARE QUITE PUT TOGETHER.
OH...
SO A GOOD PERSON...
AND THEY'RE DEPENDABLE...
HOW DEPENDABLE?
YEAH!!
I'M PRETTY SURE NOZAKI-KUN REALLY DEPENDS ON THEM!

TO THE POINT WHERE I'D LIKE TO TAKE THEIR SPOT SOME DAY...
I DIDN'T WANNA HEAR THAT...

[Extra]

BE CAREFUL

WELL... SEEMS LIKE THE BACKGROUND PERSON SHOULD WATCH OUT FOR SAKURA...

...IN A BUNCH OF WAYS...

HEY, MIKOSHIBA!

YOU HAVE SOME FREE TIME? I HAVE SOME FLOWERS I WANT YOU TO DRAW...
FOR ONE OF THE DRAMA CLUB'S BACKDROPS.
HUH!? ME!?
THAT'S REALLY KINDA SUDDEN, YOU KNOW...

IT'S AN ARCH OF FLOWERS FOR A REALLY IMPORTANT SCENE. IT'D GIVE YOUR FLOWERS THE PERFECT CHANCE TO SHINE.
C'MON, HELP ME BEWITCH THE AUDIENCE.
G— GEEZ! IF YOU INSIST! BUT JUST THIS ONCE!

MIKOSHIBA... ...YOU SHOULD PROLLY WATCH OUT FOR HORI-SENPAI...
YOU'RE TOO NAIVE...
OHHH? JEALOUS MUCH, KASHIMA?
SORRY FOR TAKING ALL OF YOUR PRAISE!!

[Extra] A TALENTED ASSISTANT FOR THE DRAMA CLUB

OKAY, SO CAN YOU DRAW A FEW FLOWERS HERE?

JUST SKETCH 'EM IN WITH PENCIL.

OH, BY THE WAY, I'M NOT GREAT AT DOING COLOR.

THAT OKAY?

YEAH, IT'S FINE.

I GOT SOMEONE ELSE FOR THAT PART.

SAKURA, HERE TO PAINT IN THE COLORS !!
REPORTING FOR DUTY!!
YOU BASICALLY ALWAYS HAVE A BRUSH ON YOU THESE DAYS...
IT'S A BIG ONE TODAY...

ギン GIN (GLINT)
ギン GIN
ギン GIN
NOZAKI-KUN'S COMING TO HELP LATER, SO LET'S START ON THE EDGES.
AND THEN, THE REMAINING CENTER PART.
OH, NOT A LOT OF ROOM HERE.
SORRY.
ぎゅう GYUU (SQUEEZE)
ぎゅう GYUU
YOU SHOULD PROLLY RESTRAIN YOURSELF A LITTLE, YOU KNOW.

SORRY, SAKURA...
IT'S A FLOWER ARCH, SO I NEED THE CENTER LEFT OPEN...
welcome!
CENTER PART
ガクッ GAKU (SLUMP)
NO WAY...!
YOU MONSTER...!
I'M PART OF AN IMPROV SESSION...!!!
※ THIS IS REAL.

[Extra]

As His Kouhai

WHATCHA UP TO, SENPAI?
DRAWING THE BACKGROUND FOR AN INDOOR SCENE.
SENPAI!

I MADE AN ENLARGED COPY OF THE BACKGROUND!
WE'RE GOING TO TRANSFER THIS, RIGHT?
!!
THAT BACKGROUND IS AMAZING...
WITH SKILLS LIKE THAT, HE COULD BE NOZAKI'S BACKGROUND PERSON...

YOU OKAY, MIKOSHIBA?
YEAH...
WAS JUST THINKING HIS BACKGROUNDS ARE PRETTY AWESOME...
CAN I SEE THAT?
SUPER-COOL, RIGHT? SENPAI'S REALLY GOOD AT THIS.
YEAH, HE IS.
I DON'T THINK YOU COULD DO ANYTHING QUITE LIKE THIS.

......WRONG!!
GIMME A WEEK, AND I'M SURE I'LL BE ABLE TO DRAW THAT WELL TOO!!
I'M HIS BELOVED, TALENTED KOUHAI, AFTER ALL!!!
I THINK YOU MIGHT ACTUALLY PULL IT OFF, BUT DON'T DO ANYTHING STUPID, OKAY?
NO ONE'S ASKING FOR THAT.

[Extra]

THEY STARTED WORKING

THEN...

...LET'S GET TO IT.

OKAY!

OH, THAT'S RIGHT.
REMEMBER WHAT NOZAKI-KUN MENTIONED THE OTHER DAY? HAVE YOU GIVEN ANY THOUGHT TO IT?
UHHH.
THE BACK-GROUND OF THE COLOR PAGE FOR THE NEXT VOLUME?
I'M FINE WITH DRAWING BUILDINGS, BUT CAN HE COLOR THEM IN?
IT'S A LOT OF DETAIL WORK.

WHAT IF WE KEPT THE NUMBER OF DIFFERENT COLORS DOWN?
MAYBE JUST THREE?
OHHH.
THAT'S ALWAYS A GOOD LOOK. IT SHOULD WORK.
THEN...
...I'LL MAKE SURE THE LINES ARE ON THE THICK SIDE.
SOUNDS GOOD!

[Extra] NO STEALING HIM

KASHI-MAAA!!!
どたどた
DOTA (THUD)
DOTA
どた
DOTA

FOR REAL!?
NO WAY!
I HAD NO IDEA!
WHAAAA!!?
DAMMIT!
THIS AGAIN!!?
WHAT ARE YOU TALKING ABOUT!!?

THE BACK-GROUND!!!
THAT BACK-GROUND!!!
BACK-GROUND...?
YOU DRAW IT LIKE THIS.
FOR REAL? NO WAY! I HAD NO IDEA!
WHAAA!?

DID YOU...
...MAKE ANY PROG-RESS...?
BEFORE I DID...?
GIRI (GRIND)
ギリッ
NO...
I'M NOT TALKING ABOUT TECHNICAL STUFF...
SORRY.

HA-HA-HA-HA-HA!
NOW WHEN I LOOK AT 'EM, THESE STICKY NOTES ARE SOOOO HORI-SENPAI!
IT'S-HORI-SENPAI!!!
YOU KNOW, JUST THE OTHER DAY YOU WERE SAYING ...
...IT SOUNDED LIKE HE WAS STALKING KASHIMA.

[ISSUE 122]

HOW SHE SEES HER CLASSMATE

RYOUSUKE-KUN'S REALLY BEEN THROWING ME OFF LATELY...

...OR SO IT FEELS ...

MIYAKO HAS BEAUTIFUL HAIR!!!

YOU HAD SOMETHING ON YOU...

THAT AND THEN THAT.

IT'S 'COS HE'S SUCH A PLAYER...
HEEEEY!
PARTY ANIMAL
?
WHAT'S UP...
...YU-KARI?

OH.
HINA-CHAN.
WHAT D'YOU THINK OF RYOUSUKE-KUN?
RYOUSUKE?
OH, HE'S SUCH A PLAYER!
MIYAKO WAS WITH A GUY!
BUT, I WON'T LOSE TO HIM!

HE'S AN HONEST WEED...
......?
ぎゅん
GYUN
ぎゅん
GYUN (WHOOSH)

THE RYOUSUKE-KUN IN MY HEAD

HINA-CHAN'S VIEW OF RYOUSUKE-KUN IS WAY TOO DIFFERENT FROM THE WAY I SEE HIM...
IT'S ODD...
HE'S DEFINITELY LIKE THIS, RIGHT...?
SAKA (SKRITCH) さか
SAKA さか

A BIT OF A PLAYBOY ...
Long hair
Works at a café
HERE'S YOUR COF-FEE.
HUH...?
BUT THAT'S NOT AS SHALLOW AS I THOUGHT ...

OH!!! BUT I HEARD THAT HE'S BEEN LEARNING HOW TO MAKE COCKTAILS LATELY, SO HE'S MORE LIKE THIS!!
I MADE THIS ORIGINAL COCKTAIL ...
... BASED... ...ON YOU. ♡
OOOH!
THERE!!! THAT'S THE PLAYBOY!!!

AND THEN IF I DO THIS ...!!!
WANT TO... ...DO BAD THINGS WITH ME?
OOOH !!!
HE IS SUCH A PLAYBOY !!!
BUT WHO IS HE ...!!?

HER INTERESTS

じっ
JI (STARE)
NOW THAT I THINK ABOUT IT, I DON'T REALLY KNOW HIM ALL THAT WELL...
IN THAT CASE...

...LET'S OBSERVE HIM!!!
ばんっ
BAN (TA-DAA)
Ryou-suke-kun
LET'S EAT... ... LUNCH.
• Talks a little rough.
• Calls class-mates by last name.
• Has a younger sister.
ALL RIGHT !!
A WEEK OF THIS SHOULD HELP A LOT...!!

A WEEK LATER
どどん
DODON (BABAM)
Today's Ryousuke-kun
Lab class day, so he dressed light.
DAYS 2-4
Today's Ryousuke-kun
Going drinking with his club
Dark
An outfit he found at a boutique that he likes
WOW ...!!!
YOU COULD ALMOST SAY I'VE MASTERED RYOUSUKE-KUN AT THIS POINT...!!!

パラ...
PARA (FLIP)
DAYS 5-7
Kind of Hawaiian
Knee-length shorts
A big bag
Looks really useful!
Accessories inside
A little ripped
Parka (Waterproof?)
!!!
RYOU-SUKE-KUN IS GONE ...!!!

BAD SAMPLE

OKAY...I FIGURED OUT HIS STYLE... BUT THAT'S NOT WHAT I NEED!!!
Daily Outfit Check
I NEED TO...
...FIND OUT WHAT SORT OF PERSON HE IS...

HAH!
THAT'S IT!!!
HOW HE ACTS AROUND WOMEN ...!!!
HEEEY. WANNA GO OUT WITH ME?
WHAA? SERIOUSLY?
PLAYBOY
?
UHH...
SO...
ACTUALLY KINDA SHY
MAYBE THAT'LL TELL ME WHAT I WANNA KNOW ...!!?

HEY.
IT'S CHIYO-CHAN!
SUMMER
OH!
HELLO, RYOUSUKE-SAN!
ARE YOU HEADING FOR WORK?

...
WHY ...?
THIS WAS SUPPOSED TO BE A SCENE OF A COLLEGE GUY...
...TALKING TO A HIGH SCHOOL GIRL...
I'M HAVING ICE CREAM TODAY.
OHHH, NICE!
...BUT IT'S SO WHOLE-SOME...

A COMMON MANGA OCCURRENCE!

I DIDN'T EXPECT THAT ONE...

WAIT... SO CHIYO-CHAN AND RYOUSUKE-KUN KNOW EACH OTHER...?

HUH?

ISN'T THAT THE GUY FROM THE CAFÉ OVER THERE?

MR. WAIT-EEER!!!
KYAAAAAA!♥
!!!
HE'S BEING SURROUND-ED BY HIGH SCHOOL GIRLS...!?
WHAAA...!?
HOW WILL HE REACT...!?

DA (DASH)
AH!!!
HE RAN...!!?
THEN... THEN THAT MEANS HE'S...!!!

C'MON, REALLY? GET LOST!
BUNCH OF BABIES!
PE (PTOOEY)
...THAT'S WHAT HE'S THINKING...
OR MAYBE...
STOPPPP! IT'S JUST TOO EMBAR-RASSING!
DAMMIT
SUMMER
...THAT'S WHAT HE'S THINKING!!!
BUT THOSE ARE COMPLETE OPPOSITES!!! I SHOULD FOLLOW THEM!!!

LETTER FROM A HIGH SCHOOL GIRL

SHE FOL-LOWED THEM.
PLEASE READ IT!!!
ばっ
BA (SHOVE)
NO MATTER HOW MANY TIMES YOU GIVE ME THAT, THE ANSWER'S THE SAME...
SUMMER
HONESTLY...
!!!

IS THAT A LOVE LETTER !!?
HE'S ACTING LIKE THAT AFTER GETTING ONE...?
PERI (PEEL)
HE REALLY IS A PLAYBOY AFTER ALL...!!!

"ABOUT THE WAITER-REQUEST SYSTEM AND COVER-CHARGE SYSTEM...
WE WANNA REQUEST KASHIMA-KUN!!
"...AND THE HAND-FED-CAKE COUPON ON THE SECRET MENU...
WE WANT KASHIMA-KUN TO DO IT!!!

"...AND ABOUT THE EXTRA OPPORTUNITY TO GO ON A DATE AFTER THE STAFF GETS OFF WORK..."
WE WANT TO GO WITH KASHIMA-KUN!!!
THIS ISN'T WHAT HIGH SCHOOL GIRLS WRITE ABOUT ...!!!

IF IT WERE A LOVE LETTER

NO WAY, NO HOW!!!
WE WORK AT A CAFÉ, YOU IDIOTS!!
OKAY, WE GET IT...
WE'LL REDO IT AND COME BACK...
JUST GIVE UP ALREADY!!!
SUMMER

HMPH!
HERE. YOU CAN HAVE THIS BACK.
TAKE IT AND GO.
ZUI (SHOVE)
IF THAT WERE A LOVE LETTER, HE'D BE A CRUEL MAN...

CAN'T YOU AT LEAST KEEP IT WITH YOU?
IT WON'T CHANGE HOW WE FEEL...!!
IF THAT WERE A LOVE LETTER, THOSE GIRLS WOULD BE SO PURE-HEARTED...

I'LL JUST PUT THIS PIC OF KASHIMA-KUN IN HERE...
...WEARING HER WORK UNIFORM.
GIMME!!!
IF THAT WERE A LOVE LETTER...
I'LL JUST PUT MY PIC IN HERE.
TAKE IT AND GO!
...THIS COULD GET GOOD!!!

HER YARDSTICK

...SO...
...I'VE BEEN OBSERVING RYOUSUKE-KUN LATELY.
WHA...?
I DIDN'T KNOW YOU AND RYOUSUKE-SAN WERE CLASSMATES...
SMALL WORLD...

HOW DO YOU SEE HIM, CHIYO-CHAN?
LET'S SEE.
HE'S LIKE AN OLDER BOY NEXT DOOR...

...is shorter than Nozaki-kun...
...and overall, he's slimmer than Nozaki-kun too.
His voice is a bit higher than Nozaki-kun's~
Tee hee! ♡
Like that ...?

OH...
SHORTER AND SLIMMER THAN NOZAKI-KUN WITH A HIGHER VOICE...
THAT'S MOST PEOPLE ...!

+RYOUSUKE-KUN

HMMM. IN THE END, I'M NOT SURE IF I'VE FIGURED OUT RYOUSUKE-KUN OR NOT...
BUT ...
NEVER MIND THAT. I REALLY NEED TO COME UP WITH MY NEXT STORY...
I'LL HAVE TO PUT THIS ON HOLD.

MY NEXT STORY ...
BOTH THE PROTAG AND HER LOVE INTEREST ARE ON THE SHY SIDE...
SO NOTHING HAPPENS...
I KNOW ...!!!
WHAT IF I ADD IN A CHARACTER KINDA LIKE RYOUSUKE-KUN?

WHATCHA DOING?
ひょいっ
HYOI (GRAB)
EEEK!
RYOU-SUKE !!!
SOMETHING LIKE THIS. IT'LL GET THE STORY MOVING...!!!
ALL RIGHT! AND IF I ADD RYOUSUKE-KUN TO THIS SCENE ...!
しゃか SHAKA (SKRITCH)
しゃか SHAKA
しゃか SHAKA

COME ON, YOU TWO !!!
STOP FUTZING AROUND IN FRONT OF THE BATH-ROOMS!!
I CAN'T GET IN!!!
!!?

ORBITAL ADJUSTMENT

NO... NOT LIKE THAT. RYOU-SUKE-KUN...
CAN YOU... GIVE IT TO HIM...!?
Kozaka-kun
OOOH—
FOR ME?
NO N— !!!
LIKE THIS... JUST LIKE THIS...

CAN YOU... GIVE THIS TO KOZAKA-KUN...!?
Kosaka-kun
HEY, COME ON! YOU SPELLED HIS NAME WRONG!!!
FIX IT!!! YOU GOTTA FIX IT!!!
RYOU-SUKE-KUN...!!!

NO... IT NEEDS TO BE MORE... LIKE HE'S TRYING TO SHAKE THINGS UP...
YOU'RE REALLY GONNA GIVE THIS TO HIM?
YOU SHOULD GO FOR ME.
I like you.
Sayuri
YES... LIKE THIS...!!!

YOU'RE REALLY GONNA GIVE THIS TO HIM?
HOW 'BOUT YOU ADD IN SOMETHING ABOUT WHY YOU FELL FOR HIM?
AND YOU REALLY GOTTA PUT YOUR FULL NAME...
I like you.
Sayuri
NO...!!!
RYOU-SUKE-KUN, NO...!!!

THE CONCLUSION HE WANTS

WHAT'S GOING ON...?
THIS CHAR-ACTER ISN'T DOING WHAT I WANT...
HAH!

WAIT, IS THIS...?
THE CHARACTERS HAVE MINDS OF THEIR OWN...
IS THIS THAT ...!!?

WOW ...!!!
THIS IS A FIRST FOR ME ...!!!
SO THIS IS RYOU-SUKE-KUN'S POWER ...!!!
IF I LET HIM DO WHAT HE WANTS ...
... WHERE IS THIS GONNA END...!?
しゃか SHAKA
しゃか SHAKA
しゃか SHAKA
SHAKA (SKRITCH)

ENOUGH ALREADY!
WITH THEM BEING SCOLD-ED.

IS HE ROUGH OR SWEET?

IT'S...
...A GAG COMEDY ...?
I'VE NEVER DONE ONE BEFORE.
BUT...
...I FINISHED MY ENTIRE ROUGH DRAFT WHILE I WAS COMING UP WITH THE STORY...
...SO I DON'T HAVE ANYWHERE TO PUT THAT LITTLE GUY...
THAT LITTLE GUY →

I GUESS I'LL MAKE RYOUSUKE-KUN CARRY HIM...
SU (FWISH)
RYOU-SUKE
WAIT!
SEE YA.

THIS BAG IS SOOOO CUTE! ♡
KYA (CHATTER)
KYA
KOSO (WHISPER)
Miyako-san, the next issue is supposed to be a wall-slam special...
!!!
OH, THAT'S RIGHT!!!

OKAY, THEN...
DON'T YOU RUN!!!
DON (THUD)
AAAAH!
YOU TOO!!
DON
EEE-EK!
MIYAKO-SAN...
...AREN'T YOU OVERUSING THIS CHARACTER ...?

HER NEW IMPRESSION

SO? DO YOU HAVE A NEW IMPRESSION OF RYOUSUKE NOW?
YOU WERE OBSERVING HIM, WEREN'T YOU?
OH!!!
I TOTALLY FORGOT ...!!!

MAYBE DON'T THINK ABOUT HIM IN A GENERAL SENSE.
JUST CONSIDER WHAT HE IS TO YOU INSTEAD.
TO ME?
TO ME, RYOUSUKE-KUN IS...

RYOUSUKE-KUN...
FOR ME, HE'S...
SEE YA.
CAN I GET...
...THREE PIECES?
DON (THUD)
...A ......

...A CONVENIENT MAN ...!!!

RYOU-SUKE-KUN...
...CAN I BUY YOU LUNCH?
WH—
WHY!?
YOU'VE BEEN WORKING REALLY HARD...
WHAT'RE YOU TALKING ABOUT!!?
...I DON'T KNOW WHAT'S GOING ON...BUT I GUESS LET'S EAT TOGETH-ER...
......
ARE YOU SURE YOU WANT TO...AFTER EVERYTHING I PUT YOU THROUGH...?
SERIOUSLY, WHAT'S THIS ABOUT?

[Extra]

THAT'S ONLY NATURAL

THIS STORY WAS REALLY FUN TO MAKE...
I THINK IT'S ALL 'COS OF RYOUSUKE-KUN.
YOU TWO BE GOOD NOW.
RYOUSUKE-KUN
HEH HEH HEH HEH.

......
....
....
....

NOOO ...!
I DON'T WANT TO SAY GOOD-BYE!!!
WAAAH!
BASA (RUSTLE)
BASA
IT CAN'T BE OVER AFTER A SINGLE CHAPTER ...!
IT'S TOO SAD...!!!

I THINK ...
...EVEN IF I FORGET THE NAME OF THE PROTAGONIST...
...I'LL NEVER FORGET RYOUSUKE-KUN'S NAME...
※HE IS A CLASSMATE ...

[Extra] A FAVORITE CHARACTER

HUH?
YOU WANT TO REUSE A CHARACTER FROM THE LAST STORY?
KOKURI (NOD)
WHAAAA?
MIYAKO-SENSEI!
YOU'VE NEVER DONE ANYTHING LIKE THIS BEFORE.

IT DOESN'T MATTER IF YOU CALL HIM A SIDE CHARACTER, HE'LL STILL STAND OUT TOO MUCH.
YOU REALLY SHOULD RETHINK THIS.
SOOO WHAT WAS HIS NAME AGAIN? KENJI-KUN?
RYOUSUKE-KUN...
IT'S THIS ONE...

MY LITTLE SIS GAVE IT TO ME.
RYOUSUKE-KUN
ON HIS PHONE
I'M REALLY GOOD AT THE CRANE GAME!
HERE, TAKE ONE.

I LIKE HIM TOO.
THIS RYOUSUKE-KUN.
LET'S MAKE HIM A REGULAR!

[Extra] A Bittersweet Turn of Events

SO ANYWAY...
...MIYAKO-SENSEI WAS BEING REALLY STUBBORN. SHE ISN'T USUALLY SO INSISTENT.
I JUST HAD TO OKAY IT.
MIYAKO-SAN WAS...? THAT'S NOT LIKE HER.

Ryousuke-kun
!
THIS MAN...
I RAN INTO HIM AT HER APARTMENT BUILDING...

SO SHE MODELED A CHARACTER AFTER A GUY SHE LIKES...?
THIS COULD GET VERY EMBARRASSING FOR HER IF HE FINDS OUT...
...BUT MAYBE IT'S A SUBTLE SIGN FROM A VETERAN ROMANCE WRITER...

NOW IT'S YOU TWO?
YOU STUPID LOVEBIRDS!!!
G—GEEZ!
RYOUSUKE...
YOU DON'T HAVE TO TEASE US...!
I'M MAD AT YOU!!!
ARE YOU TRYING TO STEAL HER FROM ME...?
WHERE'D YOU GET THAT IDEA FROM!!?
SORRY, RYOUSUKE-KUN...
WE CAN'T BE ANYTHING BUT FRIENDS...
WE'RE NOT EVEN THAT!!
IT'S A GAG COMEDY...

[ISSUE 123]

HIS CRITERIA

WHOA, NO WAY! IT'S TRAGI-LOVE!!!
TRAGIC LOVE END?
?
THE TRAGIC LOVE ENDING!!!

JUST LOOK!!!
THE MAIN GUY AND THE HEROINE ARE BOTH SLEEPING—AND THEY'LL NEVER WAKE UP AGAIN!!!
HMM?
ISN'T THAT JUST A BAD END?
YOU'D THINK SO, RIGHT!?
Mom:
"Saya...! Hiroki-kun...! Wake up...!!"

BUT THEY'RE BOTH HAVING ALL SORTS OF FUN IN THEIR DREAMS!!!
BUT IT'S DEFINITELY NOT A HAPPY ENDING EITHER!!!
YOU'RE THE PRO HERE. WHAT DO YOU THINK!?
Saya: "I'm so happy...Nothing can hurt us in here..."
We'll always be together—just the two of us.

THE BACK-GROUND IS PINK, SO...
...IT'S A HAPPY ENDING, RIGHT?
IT'S THE COLOR OF LOVE...
STUPID PRO!!!

A STEADFAST MAN

So are these tragic love endings popular or something?
WAKU (GIDDY) WAKU
WELL... I GUESS THEY HAVE THEIR FANS AND ALL...
Oh!!
Then can you teach me the basics!?

HMMM...
HE PUT HIS LIFE ON THE LINE TO SAVE THE WOMAN HE LOVES...
OH HO!
THAT'S HAPPY!
...BUT...
...SHE'S BEEN CURSED, AND THE WORLD IS RUINED.
DOON (SHOCK)
THAT'S NOT HAPPY.

IT'S FINALLY RAINING IN A VILLAGE THAT HAD A LONG DROUGHT ...
THAT'S HAPPY!
...BUT THE VILLAGERS HAD TO OFFER UP THE BLOOD OF THE HERO AND HEROINE TO MAKE IT HAPPEN.
THAT'S REALLY NOT HAPPY!!!

AFTER IT WAS DILUTED BY THE RAIN, THEIR BLOOD TURNED PINK...
MAYBE IT REALLY IS HAPPY !!!

HIS IMPRESSIONS

YOU KNOW ...
...YOU'RE BRINGING UP A LOT OF DEATH, SUFFERING, AND STUFF ABOUT THE ENTIRE WORLD...
IS THIS A FANTASY THING?
NAH. IT'S NOT LIKE...
...THEY ALWAYS HAVE TO DIE.
LET'S SEE...
SAY...

...A SUPER-JEALOUS MAN LOCKS THE HEROINE UP...
NOW YOU ...
...CAN NEVER LEAVE.
THIS CHAIN BINDING US...
...IS THE RED STRING OF FATE...
...BUT SHE AND THE GUY ARE BOTH SMILING.
JARA (RATTLE)
I'M SO HAPPY ...
NOW WE'LL ALWAYS BE TOGETH-ER...
AND THEN IT ENDS— IN THE MIDDLE OF THAT HUGE BUMMER ...

...A WORLD WHERE THEY'RE ALWAYS CHAINED TO EACH OTHER, HUH...?
IF SOMEONE TELLS YOU THAT'S HOW IT ALL ENDS...
...IT'D KINDA PISS YOU OFF, RIGHT?
YEAH, I GUESS ...
IF I WERE DRAWING IT...
IT JUST DOESN'T FEEL RIGHT...

...I'D HAVE TO EXPLAIN HOW THEY GO TO THE BATHROOM.
I NEED ...
...TO USE THE TOILET.
......!
BUT YOU JUST WENT!
I... ... HAVE DIARRHEA ...
TOILET
GEEZ ...
YOU DUMMY ...!
IT KINDA FEELS LIKE THEY'RE ENJOYING THIS.

BASED ON HIS DESIGN

THERE'S ALSO ...
...THE HEROINE WHO FORGETS EVERYTHING 'COS OF TRAUMA...
むくり
MUKURI (RISE)
EEK!
... UMM ...?
DID YOU ... ... SAVE ME?
I—
IT'S NOT MY FAULT...!!!
...AND THEN SHE ENDS UP FALLING FOR HER ABUSER AND EVEN MARRYING HIM.
THAT'S A THING TOO.

SHE'S TOTALLY HAPPY...!!! BUT THE WAY WE SEE IT, IT'S A BAD END...!!!
SO CRUEL...!!!
HMMM ...
YOU SERIOUS? YOU REALLY DON'T GET IT!!?

SUB CHARACTER
BY THE WAY, THE GUY WHO ATTACKED HER...
...LOOKS LIKE THIS.

ぐしゃあっ
GUSHAA (CRUMPLE)
SO CRUEL ...!!!
YOU GOTTA STOP JUDGING EVERYONE BY THEIR LOOKS, YOU KNOW...
YOU WOULDN'T HAVE CARED IF HE'D BEEN HOT, WOULD YOU?

AT THE VERY END

SO...
...I WANNA TRY COMING UP WITH A TRAGIC LOVE ENDING THAT'LL WORK IN A SHOUJO MANGA...
GOT IT!!!
しゅばっ
SHUBA (FWOOSH)
SHE'LL PLAY ALONG WITH PRETTY MUCH ANYTHING...

OKAY!!!
I HAVE ONE!!!
THAT WAS FAST!!!

ALL YOU GOTTA DO IS ADD A LITTLE BIT OF HAZE TO A HAPPY ENDING, RIGHT?
OKAY, HERE.
WE HAVE A NORMAL HAPPY SCENE. ALL LOVEY-DOVEY! ♡ AND THEN...
I LOVE YOU!
I'M SO HAPPY! ♡

...WE END WITH THIS PANEL.
That...
...was the happiest time of my life...
DON'T PLUNGE THEM INTO HELL IN A SINGLE PANEL!

YOU CAN'T ALWAYS GET WHAT YOU WANT

SAKURA... ISN'T THAT...
...JUST A PLAIN OLD BAD END...?
OH! YEAH, I GUESS!
THE PROTAGS HAVE TO THINK IT'S A HAPPY ENDING, DON'T THEY?
THAT'S TOUGH.

OKAY, THEN! ONE DAY, A WIZARD SHOWS UP...
...AND GIVES THE HEROINE CANDY SHE CAN EAT WITHOUT GAINING WEIGHT...
...AND A MIRROR THAT MAKES HER PRETTIER EVERY TIME SHE LOOKS IN IT.
OKAY, YEAH.
THAT SOUNDS LIKE ONE OF YOUR STORIES...
ほのぼの…
HONOBONO (HEARTWARMING)

THE HEROINE IS SUPER-HAPPY.
SHE EATS HER CANDIES AND LOOKS IN HER MIRROR EVERY DAY.
YEAH, GOOD.
THEN...
...SHE GOES TO THE MIRROR WORLD, AND A PRINCE PROPOSES TO HER...

...AND THEN IT ENDS LIKE THIS!!
FOOLISH GIRL...
THERE'S NO SUCH THING AS CANDY THAT WON'T MAKE YOU GAIN WEIGHT.
158.7
THE MIRROR USED HYPNOSIS... SO YOU DIDN'T NOTICE...
SAKURA... ARE YOU ON A STRICT DIET RIGHT NOW...?

THE NIGHT OF SLASHING SCISSORS

BUT MAYBE SOMETHING LIKE "THE WIZARD FELL FOR THE CHUBBY GIRL"...
...WOULD HAVE A SHOUJO MANGA FEEL.
HERE, EAT UP!
THERE'S LOVE THERE.
WELL ...
...IF YOU SAY SO...
WAIT A SEC!
WHAT ABOUT THE TRAGIC LOVE PART!!?

UHH.
WE JUST NEED SOMEONE TO SUFFER AS A DOWNSIDE TO ALL THIS HAPPINESS, RIGHT...?
—THEN HOW ABOUT THIS?
THE NIGHT AFTER THE TWO OF THEM GET TOGETHER ...
...HE SNEAKS OFF...
...AND ENTERS A CERTAIN LOCKED ROOM.
GII (CREAK)

...I'M SO SORRY.
MY CALCULATION WAS OFF...
DON'T HOLD IT AGAINST ME.
JAKIN (SHHNK)
!!!
STOP...!! NO MORE ...!!!
'COS OF HER, I HAVE TO...
I HAVE TO...!!!
WAIT ...!!!
IS THIS AN ENDING WHERE ANOTHER WOMAN SUFFERS ...!!?

I SHOULD LET IT OUT ANOTHER TWO INCHES.
IT WON'T FIT HER WAIST.
CHIKU (STAB)
CHIKU
CHIKU
STOP ...!!!
I'M... ALREADY ALMOST ALL PATCHES ...!!!
WEDDING DRESS
WHY DID YOU BOTH END IT WITH INANIMATE OBJECTS ...?

THAT'S THE GOAL

OH, COME ON!
YOU TWO ARE SKIMPING ON THAT SPECIAL GLOOM THAT YOU NEED FOR A PROPER TRAGI-LOVE!!
YOU DON'T HAVE THAT SENSE OF TRAGEDY ...
...THAT MAKES YOU FALL TO YOUR KNEES AND GO, "HOW DID IT COME TO THIS ...!!?"

HMMM. CAN YOU GIVE US AN EXAMPLE ...?
TRAGEDY...?
GLOOM?
......
OKAY ... LET'S USE THE TWO OF YOU...

YOU TWO ARE ROOMIES...
...BUT NOZAKI SAYS YOU DON'T HAVE TO HELP WITH ANYTHING, SAKURA...
LET ME... ...HELP YOU OUT...
...AND HE DOESN'T ASK YOU TO DO ANYTHING EITHER.
YOU HAVE DELICIOUS FOOD AND A GORGEOUS ROOM.
AND YOU'RE—USELESS AND LONELY...

......M— My happy ending ...?
WHICH PART IS!!?
We're roommates ...
THAT WAS THE FIRST LINE !!!

UNCLOUDED SIGHT

SAKURA IS NO GOOD!!!
YOU GIVE IT SOME GLOOM!!!
OKAY.
I'LL DO MY BEST!
BI (FWISH)

EVERYTHING APPEARS TO BE PEACEFUL FOR YOU TWO...
...BUT THE TRUTH IS—THIS LIFE ISN'T ALL SUNSHINE AND RAINBOWS.
IT'S TOUGH...
CAN I SKIP THE SIDE DISHES EVERY SO OFTEN...?
WHY DO I HAVE TO STRESS LIKE A HOUSEWIFE...?
I'M TIRED OF GETTING UP EARLY TO MAKE LUNCHES...

UNTIL ONE DAY, YOUR FRIENDSHIP WITH SAKURA TURNS DARK.
AND YOU CHANNEL YOUR URGES...
...INTO YOUR WORK.
BUTSU (MUTTER) BUTSU
THIS FINISHED PROJECT BECOMES YOUR MOST POPULAR PIECE YET.
CONGRATS, NOZAKI-KUN!
THANKS, BUT...
...IT BELONGS TO YOU, SAKURA...

AS LONG AS IT SELLS, I'M GOOD.
IT'S HAPPY.
AND I HELPED HIM!!
IT'S HAPPY.
THEY'RE BOTH SO SINGLE-MINDED!!!

CAN'T DENY IT

WE CAN'T GET A "THAT'S DISTURBING" VIBE FROM YOU TWO!!!
OKAY, THEM!!!
WE'LL USE THOSE TWO!!!
KASHIMA-KUN AND HORI-SENPAI ...?
D'YOU REALLY THINK YOU CAN GET THEM TO GIVE OFF THAT VIBE, THOUGH ...?

HMM, LET'S SEE...
ONE DAY...
...KASHIMA FALLS INTO A DEEP COMA.
KASHIMAAA!!!

SENPAI GRIEVES FOR HER, BUT AS HE GAZES UPON HER SLEEPING FACE, HE REALIZES A SIMPLE TRUTH—
SHE CAN'T GO ANYWHERE.
SHE'S JUST...
...SLEEPING PEACEFULLY, HERE AT MY SIDE...
THIS MIGHT JUST BE...
...MY BEST CHANCE TO BE HAPPY...

NO NEED TO LOOK SO WORRIED, Y'KNOW...
IT DIDN'T REALLY HAPPEN...

SAKIKO YUMENO'S WAY OF DOING THINGS

I'M NOT REALLY SURE ABOUT HAVING A BAD END IN A SHOUJO MANGA IN THE FIRST PLACE.

NOT A GOOD IDEA?

IT'S NICE AND IMPACTFUL, BUT IT LEAVES A BAD TASTE IN YOUR MOUTH.

THIS IS HOW I IMAGINE IT'D GO...
FIRST...
...EVERYONE'S SHOCKED BY THE UNEXPECTED ENDING, AND THERE'S ALL KINDS OF BUZZ ABOUT IT.
WOW...!!! DOES IT REALLY END LIKE THIS...!?
I DIDN'T KNOW YOU COULD WRITE STORIES LIKE THIS!
MORE...!! PLEASE SAVE THEM...!!!
SAKIKO YUMENO'S FANS ARE TOO EASY ...!!!

SO IN RE-SPONSE...
...I'D WRITE A FOLLOW-UP STORY...
AFTER THAT SHOCKING END, THEY NOW...
I'm coming to save you!
REFRAIN
SO NOW IT'S JUST A HAPPY ENDING ...!!!

AND HERE'S WHAT READERS WILL THINK!
I WISH THE STORY HAD ENDED BACK THERE.
KINDA POINTLESS?
THE STORY FEELS REALLY CHEAP NOW.
THAT'S A SAD FINISH ...!!!

AT THE END OF THE DAY...

YOU KNOW ...
...I CAN'T TELL IF I GOT THE CONCEPT ACROSS RIGHT...
MY OWN CONCEPT OF TRAGI-LOVE IS PRETTY VAGUE...
YOU THINK SO?
WE GOT IT JUST FINE, MIKORIN.
IT'S ALL GOOD!
REALLY ...?
THEN CAN YOU SUM IT UP...?

すっ...
SU (INHALE)
I'LL BE IN CHARGE OF TAKING OUT THE GARBAGE ...!!
YOU ONLY REMEMBERED THE PART ABOUT BEING ROOMIES.

C'MON, NOZAKI.
SAY SOME-THING.
HMM ......
LET'S SEE...

I'LL HANDLE THE DANGEROUS ITEMS!
WHY ARE YOU PLAYING ALONG?

MISFORTUNE THEY DIDN'T EVEN NOTICE

...So anyway, about that tragic love ending ...
UHH—
...I GET THAT YOU WANT TO WRITE A STORY LIKE THAT. HOWEVER...

...I need you to work on *Let's Fall in Love* ♡ first, please.
YOU'RE RUNNING OUT OF TIME.
OH, I'M DONE WITH MY DRAFT. I'LL SEND IT OVER!
All right. Then we'll work on your other story another time...

IT'LL NEVER WORK WITH HIS PAR-TICULAR ART STYLE ...
IT'D BE VAGUE AND FORGET-TABLE...
MAMI-KO.
THESE ARE FOR YOU.
THOSE SHOES ...!
YEAH.
HE'S MUCH BETTER WITH THIS SORT OF HAPPY STORY ...

THOSE ARE THE WHITE HEELS I'VE ALWAYS WANTED...
I'M SO HAPPY ...
LET'S GO...
...TO THE PARTY!
YEAH ...!
DOG POOP →
YUME-NOOOO !!!

TRAGIC LOVE END!!
THAT'S TOO BAD~!! THERE'S ALWAYS NEXT TIME!
IT'S NOT S'POSED TO BE LIKE THAT.
YOU'RE WAY TOO FOCUSED ON ALL THE WARM FUZZY STUFF.
HAPPY!

[Extra] YOU CAN'T ALWAYS GET WHAT YOU WANT

THE SWEET SECRET OF THE MIRROR
HIS STORY ABOUT THE WIZARD WAS LATER APPROVED.
WHAA!? YOU'RE DOING IT!!?

YEAH, THAT'S THE PLAN...
BUT SAKURA, IS IT ALL RIGHT IF I HAVE THE HEROINE GO ON A DIET?
HUH ...?
I WANT TO DO A STORY ABOUT A HEROINE WHO GAINED WEIGHT FROM EATING ALL THAT CANDY, BUT THEN MANAGES TO SHAKE OFF THE WIZARD'S INDULGENCES AND CONVEY HER OWN FEELINGS FOR HIM.
I WANT TO BE WITH YOU OF MY OWN WILL...!!!

......
OKAY! SURE!
NIKO (SMILE)
SAKURA ...!
TO BE HONEST, I JUST WANNA DO SOMETHING ABOUT HOW SHE LOOKS...
...BUT I GUESS GIRLS REALLY DO LIKE TO SEE A HEROINE WHO DOES THINGS FOR HER-SELF...

I'M FINE AS LONG AS SHE HAS TO WORK FOR THAT WEIGHT LOSS.
SAKURA ...

[Extra]

ANOTHER USE

I REALLY WISH I COULD USE THIS FOR SOMETHING, SINCE I WENT TO THE TROUBLE OF MAKING IT.
That...
...was the happiest time of my life...
THAT PAPER ONLY MAKES THINGS SUCK. GET RID OF IT ALREADY.
WHAT'S WRONG WITH YOU?

OH.
IT'S WAKAMATSU.
STOP!!!
C'MON! JUST A LITTLE BIT!
......

SU (FWISH)
すっ
That...
...was the happiest time of my life...

WHEN HE LOOKS BACK ON IT, THOSE DAYS HE HAD WITH YUZUKI WERE SO PRECIOUS...
THEY SEEM TO SHINE.
UGH! PLEASE, JUST STOP!
JUST PLAYING AROUND. NOT A CARE IN THE WORLD.
HE CAN NEVER GO BACK TO THAT TIME.
SOMEOOONE!!!
ANYOOOONE!!!

MONTHLY GIRLS' × NOZAKI-KUN

[ISSUE 124]

WE'RE GOOD FRIENDS ♡

HEY, KASHIMA.
MORN-ING.
......HUH!?

YUZUKI!!?
WHAT HAPPENED TO YOUR VOICE!!?
IT'S REALLY SCRATCHY!!
GUESS I'M COMIN' DOWN WITH SOMETHIN'. MY THROAT'S PRETTY BAD.
DON'T HAVE A FEVER, THOUGH.

THIS IS MAJOR!!!
COME WITH ME!!!
GASHI (GRAB)
KA-SHIMA...
HEH HEH HEH...
SHE'S TOTALLY PANICKING...
SUCH A DRAMA QUEEN...

SENPAI!!!
YUZUKI'S A WORSE SINGER THAN ME RIGHT NOW!!!
JUST LISTEN!!
DIE...!!!

AT ABOUT 65% OF HER POWER

IN ANY CASE, SHE SANG...

Seo

...AND WON BY A LANDSLIDE.

TAKE THAT!!!
GEHO (COUGH)
げほ
GOHO
ごほ
GAHO
がほ
BWA-HA-HA-HA!
YOU OKAY?
STILL, YOU KNOW...
...YOU MIGHT ACTUALLY BE ABLE TO SING FOR WAKAMATSU RIGHT NOW.
YOUR VOICE IS DEEPER TODAY.

BAG: COUGH DROPS

YOU THINK SO...?
YOU REALLY BELIEVE HE'LL BE ABLE TO STAY AWAKE, HORI-CHAN...?
HE ALWAYS FALLS RIGHT ASLEEP.
HMMM, YEAH...
WITH YOUR VOICE AS IT IS RIGHT NOW...

...I FEEL AS THOUGH HE'LL JUST BARELY MAKE IT—LIKE THIS.
THAT'S ROUGH.
I DON'T THINK I CAN HANDLE IT—
I'LL BURST OUT LAUGHING.

LEAVE IT TO THE DRAMA CLUB!

HEY, SO THAT MEANS NOW I CAN FINALLY SHOW WAKA WHO I REALLY AM?
HEH HEH HEH...
YEAH! FINALLY!
BUT BEFORE YOU TELL HIM...
...MAYBE DO A RUN-THROUGH FIRST!?
A RUN-THROUGH...?

SASA (BRUSH)
WE'LL PUT OUR ACTING SKILLS TO USE AND BECOME YOUNG WAKAMATSU FOR YOU.
SASA
THINK OF IT AS A REHEARSAL.
Ohhh!
SOUNDS GOOD!
JUST WAIT A MINUTE. GOTTA GET INTO THE ROLE.

BUTSU (MUTTER)
SEO-SENPAI'S LIKE THIS ALL THE TIME! ALWAYS GIVING ME TONS OF SELFISH ORDERS...
BUTSU
BUTSU
NEXT TIME I SEE HER... YEAH, NEXT TIME, I'LL DEFINITELY DO IT...!!
STOP MAKING EVERYTHING SUPER-AWKWARD RIGHT OFF THE BAT...
...HORI-CHAN.

LORELAI-SAN IS AN ANGEL.
SHE'S PURE AND INNOCENT.
SHE'S A CUTE GIRL WHO'D LOOK GREAT IN A WHITE DRESS. SHE PLAYS THE PIANO.
SHE'S GOOD AT MAKING ESCABECHE AND AMATRICIANA.
DAMMIT!!! I DON'T EVEN KNOW THOSE WORDS...
...BUT SHE SOUNDS LIKE WAKA!!!

WAKAMATSU IS LIKE THIS

WAKAMATSU (AS PLAYED BY KASHIMA)

HELLO, SEO-SENPAI!!!

DID YOU NEED ME FOR SOMETHING?

......?
WHAT'RE YOU SO EXCITED FOR...?
HUH?
YOUNG WAKAMATSU IS ALWAYS LIKE THIS.
REALLY ...?
HE'S LIKE THAT WHEN HE'S WITH YOU...?

OKAY, THEN. WAKA!!!
YOU HAVE TO LISTEN TO ME SING! RIGHT NOW!!
HUH ...!?
I JUST NEED TO LISTEN...!?
NAH. LISTEN AND TELL ME WHAT YOU THINK.
おろっ…
ORO (PANIC)
WHAT I THINK ...!?

HOW MANY PAGES DO I NEED TO WRITE ...!?
DOES PUNCTUATION COUNT FOR THE WORD COUNT!?
WHAT ABOUT PARENTHETICALS?
YOUR TAKE ON WAKA IS EXHAUSTING!

IMITATION X 2

OKAY, I'M GONNA SING...
...AND ...
HAH!
OH ...
LOOKS LIKE HORI-CHAN FIGURED IT OUT...
THAT'S WHAT HIS FACE SAYS...

SEO-SENPAI ...
... YOU'VE BEEN LYING TO ME ALL THIS TIME ...!?
GASHI (GRAB)
HUH!!?
YOU... WERE LAUGHING AT ME BEHIND MY BACK ...!!!
LORELAI-SAN NEVER EVEN EXISTED ...!!!

WAAAAAHH!
SHE NEVER EXISTED !!!
HUH ...!?
THIS IS HOW HE'S GONNA REACT ...!?
KA-SHIMA ...
WHAT ABOUT KA-SHIMA'S WAKA ...!!?

Ohhh~
You're a pretty good singer too, Seo-senpai~
WOOOW!
PACHI (CLAP)
PACHI
YOUR WAKA IS WAY TOO DUMB!!!

FOREVER OUT OF REACH

!!

THAT'S ... ...LORELAI-SAN SINGING...!!!
HER VOICE IS A LITTLE TOO DEEP, THOUGH...?
BUT...
BA (JUMP)
ばっ
...THAT'S STILL CLEARLY HER...!!!
SOMEONE IN THIS HALLWAY IS...

...LORELAI-SAN—THE PERSON I'VE ALWAYS WANTED TO MEET...!!!

THEY'RE ALL PEOPLE I JUST SAW YESTER-DAY...!!!

SENPAI'S TEACHINGS

UHHH...
WHAT'S GOING ON...?
DOES THIS MEAN...
...ONE OF THOSE THREE IS LORELAI-SAN...!!?

...I GUESS SEO-SENPAI DID SAY SHE WAS LORELAI BEFORE...
FORE-SHADOWING IS KEY.
—OR SO SENPAI SAYS.
THEN IS IT SEO-SENPAI...!!?

WAIT... NO.
AT THE END OF THE DAY, IT'S ALWAYS ABOUT LOOKS AND CHARM.
HE SAYS THAT TOO.
COULD IT BE KASHIMA-SENPAI...!!!?

BUT IT ALSO MIGHT BE THE ONE YOU LEAST SUSPECT...
IN THAT CASE, MAYBE IT'S HORI-SENPAI...!!!
ARGH...!!!
THIS MEANS IT'S AN EQUAL CHANCE OF BEING ANY ONE OF THEM, NOZAKI-SENPAI...!!!

THEY'RE UTTERLY SPEECHLESS

HAH!
WAKA-MATSU ...!!?
UM...
I'M PRETTY SURE I JUST HEARD LORELAI-SAN...
YOU HEARD THAT!!?

THE MAIN EVENT STARTED WHILE WE WERE IN THE MIDST OF OUR REHEARSAL...
NOW IT'S LIKE KASHIMA AND I ARE GETTING IN THE WAY.
THIS DOESN'T LOOK GOOD...
I HAD NO IDEA...
I CAN'T BELIEVE LORELAI-SAN...

...IS ONE...
...OF YOU ...!!!

AT LEAST NARROW IT DOWN ...!!!
WAIT...IS HE INCLUDING ME IN THERE TOO...!!?
BUT I DO KNOW IT'S ONE OF YOU THREE...!!!
HE REALLY IS...!!?

AN HONEST MAN

O-OKAY!!! I'LL JUST ASK, THEN!!!
WHICH ONE OF YOU IS LORELAI-SAN!!?

HUH...? IT'S UNANIMOUS...!!?
THIS IS...
I AM THE ONE YOU'RE LOOKING FOR.
......
THIS IS FOR THE BEST...
LADY ELLIE IS A MUCH BETTER MATCH FOR LORD ROBERT...

UMMM...
HORI-SENPAI......?
IT'S SO NICE TO MEET YOU, LORELAI-SAN.
NO MORE SHOUJO MANGA FOR YOU!
YOU NEVER MAKE ANY SENSE.

WITH ONE NOTE

...IF I SING...
...YOU'LL GET IT.
I AM LORELAI!

YEAH...
IF I SING, YOU'LL SEE...
...I CAN'T EVEN HIT THOSE NOTES.

YEAH...!
IF I SING, I'M PRETTY SURE YOU'LL GET IT...!!!

WHIRLING THOUGHTS OF YOU

WAKA!!!
NOW LISTEN UP!!!
ZA (THUD)
!

!!!
THIS IS...
...LORELAI-SAN'S VOICE...

THEN SEO-SENPAI...
...REALLY IS HER...?

SEO-SENPAI IS...
HEY... ...WAKA.
DIDJA KNOW THAT CHARRED NEWT'S A THING...?
I WONDER... ...IF IT'S ANY GOOD.
I FOUND A GECKO THE OTHER DAY, YOU KNOW.
D'YOU THINK YOU... ...CAN EAT THEM?
AND THERE'S FROGS TOO.
WHY DID I REMEMBER THAT SCENE JUST NOW?

TRUST ME!!

I'M LORELAI! LORELAI!!!
I!!! AM LORELAI!!!
<LORELAI>...?
THAT'S RIGHT!!! YOUR BELOVED LORELAI!!!

THAT VOICE YOU LISTEN TO EVERY NIGHT WHEN YOU GO TO BED!!!
THAT VOICE YOU LOVE AND THANK ALL THE TIME! THE PERSON YOU SEE AS AN ANGEL SENT FROM HEAVEN!
THAT'S ME!!!
LORELAI-SAN IS DIVINE!

!!!
...THEN THAT MEANS...!!!
THE PERSON WHO PUT ME TO SLEEP FOR A LAUGH AND...
...THEN MESSED WITH ME WHILE I WAS OUT...
...WAS YOU, SEO-SENPAI...!!?
GUSHA (CRUMPLE)

THAT...
...WAS SOMEONE ELSE, FOR SURE...
WHO'S THIS LORELAI PERSON...?
SHE...
...IS TRYING TO HAVE IT BOTH WAYS...!!!
THAT'S DIRTY!!!

IT FEELS REAL

THAT NIGHT
OKAY ...
TIME FOR BED.
PI (BEEP)
ピッ

HUH...? WAIT A MINUTE.
DIDN'T SOMEONE SAY SOMETHING ABOUT SEO-SENPAI BEING LORELAI-SAN TODAY...?
UTO (DOZE)
うと…
Lorelai-san
SO THIS ...
...IS SEO-SENPAI SINGING ...?
......

WAAAAAAAH!
GABBAA (JUMP)
ガッばぁ

OH, I GET IT.
NOW THAT HE KNOWS IT'S YUZUKI, WHEN HE LISTENS...
...IT'S JUST... YOU KNOW.
TOO REAL...?
I GUESS IT'S LIKE HAVING SOMEONE YOU KNOW WHISPERING RIGHT IN YOUR EAR...
OKAY, KASHIMA.
SING.
PI
WHY? WELL, I GUESS I CAN GIVE IT A TRY FOR YOU...
NOT LIKE I MIND.

[Extra]

SLEEP-LEARNING

HE TRIED TO SLEEP WITH IT.
WAKU (GIDDY) わく
WAKU わく
ALL RIGHT!
I'M GONNA FALL ASLEEP LISTENING TO THIS TONIGHT!

......

THIS IS BAD, KASHIMA!!! THIS RECORDING IS A HAZARD TO MY HEALTH!!!
THE ONE OF YOU SINGING!!!
HUH? WHAT D'YOU MEAN? DID YOU GET TOO EXCITED OVER ME WHISPERING TO YOU?

MY PITCH IS ALL OVER THE PLACE WHEN I SING THIS SONG NOW!!!
SO MY TONE DEAFNESS IS CONTA-GIOUS...?

[ISSUE 125]

HIS REPORT AND THEIR REACTIONS

WHAT... DID YOU JUST SAY, WAKAMATSU...?
UH... SO...
LORELAI-SAN... IS SEO-SENPAI...

A-ARE YOU SAYING THAT FOR REAL, WAKAMATSU!!?
"YUZUKI IS LORELAI!"
THAT'S WHAT YOU JUST SAID, RIGHT!!?
THEY'RE BOTH SURPRISED TOO...!!!
I MEAN, OF COURSE THEY ARE... IT'S DEFINITELY SHOCKING...!!!

NO WAY...!! HE ACTUALLY REALIZED...!!?
YOU'RE NOT GOING TO GO BACK AND SAY YOU ACTUALLY MEANT RYOUSUKE-SAN, ARE YOU...!?
I KNOW HOW YOU WORK!!
HUH...?
WHY DO THEY LOOK SO SERIOUS...?

I CAN'T BELIEVE YOU HAD A BIG REVEAL WITHOUT ME AROUND TO SEE IT...!!!
GIRII (GRIND)
AND YOU, SENPAI...
WHAT'S THAT LOOK FOR...!?

RIGHT IN FRONT OF HIS INNOCENT KOUHAI

UM!
I'M PRETTY SURE SEO-SENPAI ...
...WASN'T HIDING IT TO BE MEAN OR ANYTHING ...
YOU DON'T HAVE TO GET SO MAD...
HE'S SO SWEET.
SO PURE.

WHAT SORT OF FEELINGS ARE BEHIND YOU SAYING THAT...?
TELL SENPAI THE WHOLE TRUTH.
WHAT GIVES YOU THE RIGHT TO ASK THAT ANYWAY?

BE THAT AS IT MAY, I'M STILL KINDA CONFUSED ...
...SO I JUST WANTED TO TELL ALL OF YOU...!
YOU DO KNOW IT'S ALL RIGHT TO WORRY FOR A BIT LONGER, RIGHT!!?
IT'S REALLY IMPORTANT!!
WHENEVER I THINK ABOUT HOW LORELAI-SAN IS REALLY SEO-SENPAI ...
... PUTTING IN MY EARBUDS MAKES ME FEEL... REALLY WEIRD!
IT'S OKAY!!! YOU DON'T HAVE TO TELL US ALL OF THAT!!!
YOU'RE JUST TOO PURE!!

OHHH...?
SU (FWISH)
ARE YOU HEARTLESS OR WHAT!?

AN INANE CONVERSATION

YOU WANT TO TALK ABOUT IT WITH OTHER PEOPLE AND REALLY FIGURE IT OUT, DON'T YOU, WAKAMATSU?

I GET IT.

I'M PRETTY SURE I DO...

YEAH...

...I GUESS...

WHA...? YOU DO...?

I GUESS I GET IT...

WHAT'S WITH THESE BLOCK-HEADS...?

SO WHAT...
...D'YOU THINK OF SEO ANYWAY?
HE JUMPED RIGHT TO THE FINALE...!!!

HUH...? UHHH...
I'VE ALWAYS HAD A THING FOR LORELAI-SAN, AND THEN SHE SAID SHE'S HER.
I'M NOT SURE WHAT TO THINK NOW...
SEE? HE'S TOTALLY BAFFLED!!! SAY SOMETHING!!!

I GET IT...
IF YOU THOUGHT SOMETHING WAS BURDOCK ROOT JUST THE DAY BEFORE...
...AND THEN YOU FIND OUT IT'S ACTUALLY SHIITAKE MUSHROOMS, THAT'S PRETTY CONFUSING, ISN'T IT...?
YOU'RE THE WORST...
...AT COMING UP WITH EXAM-PLES!!!

WHEN YOU MIX TWO EMOTIONS

UMMM...

OKAY, SO WE KNOW THAT YOU REALLY LOVE LORELAI-SAN.

BUT WHAT D'YOU THINK OF YUZUKI ...?

HUH ...?

I GUESS IF I HAVE TO SAY...I'M NOT A FAN...?

SOMETHING LIKE THAT...?

HMM.

WHEN YOU LEARN THE PERSON YOU LOVE IS SOMEONE YOU'RE NOT A FAN OF...

NOT A FAN
LOVE
PAAN (BLAM)
THE VOID ......?
THEY CANCEL EACH OTHER OUT ...!!?

IT'S LIKE THIS...
NO, EMOTIONS ...
...DON'T JUST CRASH INTO EACH OTHER LIKE THAT.
NOT A FAN
LOVE
KYU
KYU (SQUEAK)
I SEE!!
SO THE COMBO OF THE TWO IS SOME NEW EMOTION!!!
HEH HEH HEH.
THAT'S RIGHT...

NOT A FAN
LOVE
HATRED
WHY !!?

WHEN HE SEES HER

BUT THEN...
...HOW DO I ACTUALLY FEEL ABOUT SEO-SENPAI...?
NOOO IDEA.
JUST GO AND SEE HER...

HE'S RIGHT, WAKAMATSU-KUN.
WHAT YOU FIRST THINK WHEN YOU SEE HER...
...IS...
...HOW YOU REALLY FEEL... ♡
SAKURA-SENPAI...!!!

YES...
LIKE THIS...
SEO-SENPAI!
...THE PERSON I'VE ALWAYS ADORED, SHE'S LORELAI-SAN... ...
WAKA?
WHAT DO I DO...?
I LOVE HER...!!
DOKIN (BADUM)

SEO-SENPAI!
SHE'S LORELAI-SAN...
...BEEN LYING TO ME... SHE'S ...
I'LL NEVER FORGIVE YOU...!!!
SERIOUSLY? IT'S OBVIOUS HE'S GONNA ATTACK HER ON SIGHT LIKE THAT.
WHAT'S WITH THAT EQUIPMENT...?

THE REACTION SHE EXPECTED

THE NEXT DAY
HEY, CHIYO.
I TOLD WAKA ABOUT BEING LORELAI THE DAY BEFORE YESTERDAY...
!!!!...
WE WERE JUST TALKING ABOUT THAT...!!!

...AND HE JUST KINDA ACCEPTED IT AND LEFT...
OKAY, BYE!
Y-YEAH...
WHAT'S WITH HIM...?
SHE'S DISAPPOINTED...!!!
THAT'S SO CUTE!!!

I KNOW, RIGHT!!? HE REALLY SHOULD HAVE BEEN MORE SHOCKED!!!
YOU SHOULD SAY THAT!!!
HUH...? TO WHO...?
I KNOW, RIGHT!!?
I MEAN, HE KNOWS YOU'RE LORELAI-SAN NOW!!!

HUH? WHA? NO WAAAAY! WAIT A MINUTE! YOU'RE LORELAI-SAN!?
WAIT. NO, I CAN'T!
WAIT!
AHHHHHH!!!...
THAT'S THE SORT OF REACTION YOU WANTED, ISN'T IT!!?
YOU SHOULD SAY SO!!!
I DON'T WANT THAT MUCH.

HER LINGERING INFLUENCE

!!!

THAT'S ...

...SAKURA-SENPAI AND SEO-SENPAI ...!!!

ALL RIGHT!!!

I'M GONNA GO SEE HER!!!

SEO-SENPAI!!

HMM?

WHAT YOU THINK WHEN YOU FIRST SEE HER...

SEO-SENPAI
• CRUEL
• ALWAYS ORDERING ME AROUND
LORE-LAI-SAN
• KIND, ANGELIC
• WOULD DO ANYTHING FOR HER

ZA (FWOOSH)
I SHALL CARRY YOUR BAG FOR YOU!!!
BIKU (STARTLE)
BIKU
HUH?
WHY ...!!?

HOW HE FEELS RIGHT NOW

WHY DID YOU DO THAT, WAKAMATSU-KUN...?

KU (SINK)

I...

...REALIZED SOMETHING WHEN I SAW HER FACE A MOMENT AGO...

I CAN'T DEFY SEO-SENPAI...
IT'S BETTER TO JUST DO WHAT SHE SAYS...
YOU WERE REALLY THINKING SOMETHING SO SAD...?

AND LORELAI-SAN...LORELAI-SAN HAS BEEN MY SAVIOR. I OWE HER...
I WANT TO SHOW HER HOW GRATEFUL I AM...
YOU WERE REALLY THINKING ABOUT YOUR OBLIGATIONS...?

AND...
...I JUST REALIZED THAT I'VE TALKED TO LORELAI-SAN A WHOLE BUNCH, THROUGH SEO-SENPAI!!!
AAAAAAHHHH!
I WISH YOU'D REALIZED THAT TWO DAYS AGO!!!
NOT RIGHT NOW!!!!

THE PERSON INSIDE

OH, I GET IT...SO THE REASON YOU LEFT THE OTHER DAY IS 'COS YOU'RE REALLY THAT THICK...?
I MEAN, I AM LORELAI.
YEAH, THAT'S IT...
YOU WOULDN'T JUST LEAVE LIKE THAT NORMALLY ...
'COS I'M LORELAI.
THIS WAS REALLY BUGGING HER...

OKAY.
LORELAI-SAN'S GONNA SHAKE YOUR HAND.
WHA?
OH!
OKAY!!!
THANKS SO MUCH!!
CAN'T SAY NO, CAN YOU?
AFTER ALL, YOU LOOOOVE LORELAI SO MUCH.
HA! HA! HA!

WAKAMATSU-KUN?
YOU GOT TO SHAKE LORELAI-SAN'S HAND.
HOW DO YOU FEEL?
IT'S LIKE I'M GETTING REALLY EMOTIONAL...
I THINK ...

...THIS IS THE SAME SORT OF FEELING YOU GET WHEN...
...YOU SHAKE YOUR FAVORITE CHARACTER'S HAND AT A THEME PARK...
EH HEH HEH HEH.
BUT THE PERSON INSIDE ISN'T REAL...

AN ADORABLE WORLD

OH...!
CAN I HAVE YOUR AUTO-GRAPH ...!?
HA HA HA!
OKAY, SURE.
SHE LOOKS REALLY HAPPY.
I WONDER WHAT LORELAI-SAN'S SIGNATURE IS LIKE...
Lorelaj
THIS, MAYBE?

キュッ
KYU (SQUEAK)
Yuzuki "Lorelai" Seo
!!!
SHE'S INSISTING ON USING HER REAL NAME!!!

WHA...!? IS YUZUKI MAD!?
IS SHE ANNOYED THAT HE'S ONLY SAYING NICE THINGS ABOUT LORELAI!?
!!
OH... HE JUST REALIZED IT!!
ISN'T THAT CUTE!? SHE'S SO PURE. IT'S ADORABLE!!
RIIIIIGHT!!?

HUH ......?
IT'S REALLY YOUR NAME ...?
YOUR MIDDLE NAME IS LORELAI ...?
HE'S SO PURE TOO!!!

LORELAI ATTACK

U-UM... SEO-SENPAI... THERE'S ACTUALLY SOMETHING ...
...I...
...WANTED TO ASK LORELAI-SAN...IF I EVER MET HER...
もじ もじ
MOJI MOJI (FIDGET)
C'MON, REALLY? YOU'RE NOT GONNA ASK ME TO PUT ON A WHITE DRESS AND SING YOU HYMNS, ARE YOU?
NO...TO TELL THE TRUTH...

ぐしゃあっ
GUSHAA (CRUMPLE)
どんっ
DON (THUD)
カチッ
KACHI (CLICK)

ぐー
GUUU (ZZZ)
TIME TO IMPACT...
14.06 SECONDS.
I KNEW IT.
HE GOES DOWN EVEN FASTER WITH SLOW SONGS.
スッ
SU (FWISH)
I'LL TRY SOME ROSSINI NEXT.

REALITY AND PROPORTIONALITY

YOU REALLY ARE LORELAI-SAN...
しみじみ...
SHIMIJIMI (AWESTRUCK)
AND YOU REALLY ARE AN ATHLETE...
YOU SOUND SARCASTIC...

SENPAI IS LORELAI-SAN... SENPAI IS LORELAI-SAN...
WE'RE STARTING ON A NEW SONG IN GLEE CLUB.
OKAY ...
I THINK IT'S FINALLY STARTING TO FEEL REAL...

I WAS ALL FLUSTERED TWO DAYS AGO...
...BUT IT SEEMS LIKE NOW I'LL FINALLY BE ABLE TO RELAX AGAIN...
HA HA HA.
SEO-SENPAI IS LORELAI-SAN...
カチッ
KACHI

ぶちっ
BUCHI (YANK)
WAAAAAAHHH!
HE NO LONGER USES HEADPHONES.

HE SWITCHED TO
SPEAKERS INSTEAD.

[Extra]

RESPONSE TIME

...YOU WERE LASTING A LITTLE LONGER BEFORE YOU FELL ASLEEP, RIGHT?
SO ...
DID YOU BUILD SOME RESISTANCE?
HUH?
YOU REALLY THINK SO?
I WONDER WHY.
GASA (RUSTLE)

HEEEY, WAKA!
IT'S LORELAI-SAMA!!
!

SEO-SENPAI..? WAIT... NO... THIS IS LORELAI-SAN...
CHI (TICK)
CHI
CHI
CHI
SEO-SENPAI IS LORELAI-SAN. SHE WAS DOING ALL OF THOSE THINGS BEFORE, SO......
OH, SO THAT'S HOW IT IS.

BATAN (THUD)
ばたんっ
ぐー
GUUU (ZZZ)
OH...
IT'S JUST HIS BRAIN TAKING LONGER TO PROCESS THINGS NOW...

[Extra]

FOR LORELAI-SAN

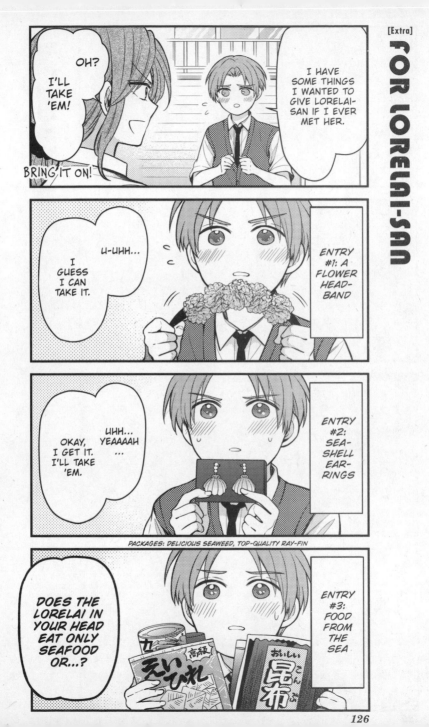

I HAVE SOME THINGS I WANTED TO GIVE LORELAI-SAN IF I EVER MET HER.
OH?
I'LL TAKE 'EM!
BRING IT ON!

ENTRY #1: A FLOWER HEAD-BAND
U-UHH...
I GUESS I CAN TAKE IT.

ENTRY #2: SEA-SHELL EAR-RINGS
UHH... YEAAAAH ...
OKAY, I GET IT. I'LL TAKE 'EM.

PACKAGES: DELICIOUS SEAWEED, TOP-QUALITY RAY-FIN

ENTRY #3: FOOD FROM THE SEA
DOES THE LORELAI IN YOUR HEAD EAT ONLY SEAFOOD OR...?
高級
えいひれ
おいしい
昆布

[Extra]

MERMAID-SENPAI

WELL, LORELAI-SAN?
むしゃむしゃ
MUSHA (MUNCH)
MUSHA
I LIKE THE SNACKS THE BEST.
THIS CRAB'S PRETTY GOOD.

SO D'YOU FINALLY GET IT? I'M LORELAI.
I... THINK SO...
NOW THAT I CONSIDER IT, I GUESS A SMALL PART OF ME MUST'VE SUSPECTED YOU WERE MAYBE HER...

HUH...
YEAH, MAKES SENSE.
CAN'T HIDE MY OVERWHELMING BEAUTY AND TALENT, AFTER ALL...

I MEAN, LOOKING BACK, YOUR LEGS ARE ALWAYS BARE...
THAT SHOULD'VE CLUED ME IN.
MY LEGS AREN'T BARE 'COS I JUST CAME OUT OF THE SEA, YOU KNOW.

[Extra]

NO FEWER WORRIES

SO WHAT ENDED UP CHANGING BETWEEN THEM?
ANYTHING?
UMMM, LET'S SEE.

WAKAMATSU-KUN'S STARTED APPROACHING YUZUKI ON HIS OWN ACCORD.
OH...?
THAT'S A HUGE CHANGE.
NOTHING TO WORRY ABOUT THERE, THEN.

AND...
...HE'S GOTTEN MORE PROACTIVE ABOUT DOING WHAT SHE SAYS.
HEY, SHE'S MAKING YOU CARRY HER BAG.

AND HE DOESN'T PUSH BACK WHEN SHE GOES OVERBOARD ANYMORE.
YOU NEED TO TELL HER WHEN YOU CAN'T DO IT, WAKAMATSU!!!
A PIGGY-BACK RIDE TOO IS A BIT MUCH!!!

LOVE
[ISSUE 126]

PICK YOUR OWN THEME

WHA?
WE GET TO PICK OUR OWN THEMES FOR OUR...
...NEXT HOME EC CLASS?

YEAH.
WE'RE SUPPOSED TO COME UP WITH ONE IN OUR GROUPS.
EVERYONE'S ALREADY WORKING ON THEIRS.
OOOH !!!
I WONDER WHAT SORT OF THEMES PEOPLE ARE GONNA GO WITH.

YUMI-CHAN SAID HER GROUP IS DOING "Stuff I want my boyfriend's mom to make for me."
YEP.
TITLE:
MOM'S FEAST ♡
I'M PRETTY SURE NONE OF THEM HAVE BOY-FRIENDS, THOUGH.
GEEZ!
THEY'RE GETTING AHEAD OF THEM-SELVES!!
AH HA HA HA HA!

AND TAKAHAMA-KUN'S GROUP IS GONNA DO "Stuff you wanna make after a fight with your little sister."
TITLE:
SORRY, MY ANGEL
EGGS
OMELET RICE
FORGIVE ME!
I DON'T THINK ANY OF THEM HAVE LITTLE SISTERS, THOUGH.
ISN'T THAT KINDA CREEPY?

MY OFFBEAT FRIENDS

SHOULDN'T THESE THEMES BE MORE, Y'KNOW...
..."MEAT DISHES" OR "EGG DISHES" ...?
THESE ARE BASICALLY FULL SENTENCES.
BUT THOSE ARE LESS OF A THEME AND MORE OF A CATEGORY, AREN'T THEY?
NO, BUT...
...IT'S JUST WEIRD.

YOU TELL THEM, MISAKI-CHAN!!!
IF EVERYONE ELSE WANTS TO GO WITH AN OFFBEAT ONE, THEN I'LL PLAY ALONG.
LET'S DO A FULL-SENTENCE THEME.
YOU SEEM WEIRDLY OKAY WITH THIS!!!

I KNOW! LET'S GO WITH "STUFF YOU CAN MAKE IN FIVE MINUTES"!
THE PERFECT PLAN!!
THEN WHAT WOULD WE DO FOR THE OTHER NINETY-FIVE MINUTES ...!!?

!
THEN "STUFF YOU CAN MAKE IN JUST A HUNDRED MINUTES"!
HOW 'BOUT THAT!?
IT'S PERFECT!!!
THAT'S THE ONE THEME WE'RE ALL SHARING !!!
'COS IT'S A CLASS!!!

THEMED FOOD ♡

OH, THAT'S RIGHT. YOU AND WAKAMATSU-KUN ARE PRETTY CLOSE, RIGHT, YUZUKI?
YEP.
WE ARE!
THEN... ...HOW ABOUT THIS?

OUR THEME IS...
..."FOOD THAT WOULD MAKE AN OVERLY SINCERE BASKETBALL PLAYER FALL FOR YOU IN AN INSTANT! ♡"
IT SOUNDS KINDA NASTY WHEN YOU PUT IT LIKE THAT.

OH, OH, OH, OHHHH! NOZAKI-KUN!!!
BA (FWOOSH)
I WANNA MAKE SOMETHING FOR NOZAKI-KUN!!!
THAT'S IT!!
OHHH—
NOZAKI-KUN, HUH~ HOW ABOUT THIS?

THE THEME IS...
..."EASY DISHES TO GET THE BORING, PLAIN GUY IN YOUR CLASS IN THE MOOD. ♡"
ADDING A HEART DOESN'T FIX EVERYTHING, YOU KNOW.

SO, BASICALLY...

LET'S JUST ASK HIM, THEN!
NOZAKI-KUN, IF WE MADE YOU SOMETHING IN HOME EC, WHAT WOULD YOU WANT?

IN HOME EC...?
SOME SORT OF DESSERT, I GUESS?
EVEN IF YOU DON'T COOK EVERY DAY LIKE I DO...
...MOST PEOPLE CAN HANDLE THAT...
I'LL MAKE THESE FOR SUZUKI-KUN!

WAIT.
A SIMPLE MISTAKE WOULD BE NICE TOO.
THEY'RE BURNED!!!
DISASTER!
THEN ...
...YOU CAN EAT THEM ANYWAY AND SAY, "IT'S ALL RIGHT. THEY'RE DELICIOUS."
HAPPY!!
I SEE!!

THEME:
"SOME HYPOTHETICAL DISH THAT CAN SOOTHE THE PRIDE OF SOMEONE WHO CALLS HIMSELF A GOOD COOK. ♡"
BUT DELIBERATELY MESSED UP!!
THAT'S NOTHING BUT MALICE!!!

A CERTAIN U.N.

OKAY, FINE...
THEN LET'S GO WITH *"A treat for Chiyo Sakura's crush."*
KARI (SKRITCH)
KARI
NOT REALLY HIDING HER PERSONAL INFO, ARE YOU...?
NOT THAT I REALLY CARE...

HEY, TAKEDA!
WHAT'S YOUR GROUP DOING?
...OH!
AHH.
HE SEEMS...
...LIKE THE KIND OF GUY WHO'S INTO TRADITIONAL JAPANESE SWEETS.
LIKE, MAYBE SOMETHING MATCHA FLAVORED?

HUH...
HE'S PRETTY TALL, SO I BET HE LOVES DAIRY PRODUCTS.
MAYBE CHEESE-CAKE?
I'VE GOT THIS GREAT RECIPE BOOK.

BUT, Y'KNOW, NOZAKI...
SO NOZAKI-KUN...
NOZAKI WOULD...
CAN'T YOU AT LEAST STICK TO HIS INITIALS!!?

I'LL SURPRISE YOU

...SO THAT'S HOW IT WENT...
HUH ...? YOUR ENTIRE CLASS KNOWS ...?
THAT'S ROUGH.
2-G
OH! SPEAKING OF WHICH, OUR CLASS ALREADY DID IT.
WE HAD HOME EC.

HUH?
WHAT WAS YOUR THEME!? WHAT SORT OF THINGS DID YOU MAKE!?
I FEEL LIKE YOU'D PICK SOMETHING AMAZING!
"A DESSERT TO SURPRISE THE RECIPIENT" IS... ...WHAT WE WENT WITH.
OHHH!
HOW SO!?

WE MADE A... ...CHOCOLATE LAVA CAKE.
YOU CUT IT OPEN, AND CHOCOLATE OOZES OUT.
DOROOO (OOZE)
OH! I HAVE A PIC.
GOSO GOSO (RUMMAGE)
I'M PRETTY SURE I HAVE A COPY OF WHAT WE TURNED IN...

FOUND IT!
HERE IT IS.
THEME: "A DESSERT TO SURPRISE THE RECIPIENT"
TITLE: YOUR GUTS
WAIT! WHAT'S WITH THAT TITLE?

HE SAW THAT COMING

SAKURA'S MAKING A DESSERT FOR HOME EC.

YEAH, I KNOW!

SHE SAID THEY WERE GONNA MAKE SOME KINDA COOKIES.

COOK-IES, HUH ...?
I HOPE SHE DOESN'T BURN HERSELF WHEN SHE USES THE OVEN...
CHIKU (STAB)
ちく
CHIKU
ちく
CHIKU
ちく
YOU SHOULD PROBABLY BE MORE WORRIED ABOUT FINISHING YOUR MANGA...
YOU DON'T REALLY HAVE TIME TO BE SEWING THAT, Y'KNOW.

THE NEXT DAY
I KNOW, I KNOW!
YOU GOT THOSE FROM NOZAKI, RIGHT?
GOOD FOR YOU.

YOU REALLY SHOULD USE THOSE!
STORAGE
GAPO (SLIDE)
がぽっ

LOOKING FORWARD TO CLASS A

OKAY, EVERYONE. ARE YOU ALL SET?
HOME EC
PLEASE FOCUS ON GETTING YOUR DISHES DONE WITHIN THE ALLOTTED TIME.
CLASS A... THEY'RE A SERIOUS, LOW-MAINTE-NANCE CLASS...
OH MY. YOU'RE MAKING HAMBURGERS, FRIED CHICKEN, AND STEAK ROLLS...
QUITE A BIT OF MEAT.
HEE HEE HEE.
WHAT'S YOUR THEME?

"IT'S GOOD, BUT IT'S ALL SO BROWN!!
"BOYS JUST NEVER THINK ABOUT COLOR!
"HON-ESTLY ~!!"

'COS NO ONE LIKES YOU IF YOU'RE A SUPER-GREAT COOK.
IT'S REALLY IMPORTANT TO HAVE A WEAK SPOT!
HA-HA-HA-HA-HA!
THESE BOYS ARE SLY...

LET'S DECORATE THEM

THE GROUP DOING THE THEME "COOKIES FOR CHIYO SAKURA'S CRUSH."
MAKING THE COOKIE DOUGH WAS PRETTY EASY...
CAN WE REALLY STRETCH THIS OUT FOR TWO HOURS...?
WE'RE GOOD.
DECORATING 'EM WILL TAKE A BUNCH OF TIME.
THAT'S THE IMPORTANT PART.

HE'S YOUR CRUSH, SO...
...LET'S GIVE THEM A THEMATIC LOOK!
LOTS OF HEARTS.
I YOU
LOVE
LIKE LIKE
OH, THAT MAKES SENSE!!

WOULDN'T IT BE CUTE IF WE PUT HIS NAME ON THEM?
野崎
NOZAKI
野
NO
崎
ZAKI
梅
UME
太
TA
郎
ROU
野崎
NOZAKI
WHY ARE THEY ALL KANJI...?

WE WANNA MAKE HIM FEEL OKAY ABOUT THIS, SO WE SHOULD ACTUALLY WRITE IT.
安心です
YOU'RE OKAY
安全
SAFE
食べても OK
EAT ME IT'S OK
おいしいよ
I'M TASTY
THAT SEEMS REALLY SKETCHY...

BASKETBALL CLUB

WHY DON'T YOU GIVE SOME TO WAKA-MATSU-KUN, YUZUKI?
HMM?
HUH... YEAH, I GUESS...
OKAY, THEN I'LL...
...MAKE SOME FOR MY LITTLE BRO!
HIRO-KUUUUN!

若
WAKA
MATSU
松
HIRO
博
竹
TAKE
DA
田
HIRO
広
WHY ARE THEY ALL KANJI...!!?

WE SHOULD MAKE THEM CUTER...
I KNOW!
WHY DON'T WE MAKE SOME THAT LOOK LIKE BASKET-BALLS!?
THAT SHOULD BE EASY!!
BA (FWIP)
ばっ
OH YEAH.
LET'S TRY IT.

SORRY...
YOU CAN KEEP WRITING KANJI ON THEM...
THE KANJI AREN'T COMING OUT RIGHT EITHER...

CHIYO COOKIES

OKAAAAY!
ALL DONE!!!
Oh!
What's with those faces? They're so cute!!

THE THEME IS A CRUSH, SO I DECIDED TO MAKE REACTION SHOTS TOO~!
YOU'RE TALKING LIKE IT'S NOT ABOUT YOU.
THIS IS "HE TOOK THEM! ♡"
AND THIS IS "HE REFUSED THEM..."

WHAT ABOUT THIS?
"WHAT IF HE GETS HOW I FEEL, BUT TRIES TO REJECT ME BY JUST KIND OF AVOIDING ME STARTING TOMORROW...?"
THIS COOKIE'S REALLY GOING THROUGH A LOT...

THEN...
...WHAT ABOUT THIS ONE?
"MISAKI-CHAN GAVE HIM COOKIES BEFORE I COULD...WHY WOULD SHE DO THAT...?"
LEAVE ME OUT OF THIS!

SHE'S FROZEN

OH, WE MIGHT WANT THE TEACHER TO TAKE A LOOK AT THEM!!
LET'S LINE THEM ALL UP!!!
"COOKIES FOR CHIYO SAKURA'S CRUSH"...?
NOW THEY'RE JUST BEING MEAN...

きちっ…
KICHI (ASSEMBLED)
NO ZAKI UME TA ROU
野崎梅太郎
DON'T LINE THEM UP LIKE THAT...!!!
IT MAKES IT OBVIOUS!!!

HEY, LOOK.
DON'T YOU THINK ...
...THEY'RE A LITTLE OVER-DECORATED?
THEY TOTALLY ARE.
THAT ICING'S REALLY THICK...
THEY'RE KINDA EXTRA.
THAT'S ALL YOU HAVE TO SAY!!?

I HAD A BIT OF HARD TIME GETTING THE CHARACTER FOR "ZAKI" TO COME OUT RIGHT...
TEE HEE...
YOU'RE OKAY WITH THIS TOO!!?

WRAPPED UP

OH, THAT'S RIGHT.
I'VE NEVER GIVEN NOZAKI-KUN ANY HOMEMADE FOOD BEFORE...
I HOPE IT WORKS OUT...
DOKI (BADMP) DOKI DOKI
HUH? THE VERY FIRST COOKIES YOU MADE FOR HIM HAVE YOUR FACE ON THEM?
YOU'VE GOT GUTS!

I'M PRETTY SURE YOU CAN JUST SORTA GIVE THEM TO HIM...
"YOU HUNGRY? WANT SOME OF THESE?" ALONG THOSE LINES.
N—
NOZAKI-KUN!!!

ARE YOU HUNGRY!!?
DO YOU WANNA EAT THESE!!?
DO YOU WANNA EAT SWEETS!!?
WHAT-EVER'S FINE. JUST— DO YOU WANNA EAT!!?

BOX: CHOCOLATE

WHAT'S THE POINT OF HIM GIVING YOU THINGS?

BALTIMORE COUNTY
PUBLIC LIBRARY

bcpl.info

Storytelling Through Classical Indian Dance

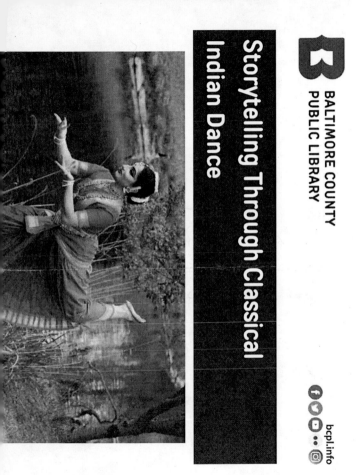

poor puppy kitty

bad

4days

410 262 68 40

Brandon Coulson

THE SECRET MESSAGE

NO-ZAKI-KUN!!!

H-HERE! THIS IS HOW I FEEL!!!

BA (SHOVE)

ばっ

OH.

FOR ME? THANKS, SAKURA.

HEY, DID YOU EVER EAT THOSE COOKIES SAKURA GAVE YOU?

KASHIMA TOLD ME ABOUT THEM.

NO...

AFTER SHE SAID HER FEELINGS ARE IN HERE, I—

WHAT IN THE WORLD COULD IT BE...?

WHA...?

JUST OPEN THEM.

GOSO (RUMMAGE)
......!
LETTERS ...?
OH, IF I LINE THEM UP LIKE THIS...

THIS IS HOW SAKURA FEELS—
太
T
T
A
I GOT FAT
"...FAT" ...
"I GOT...
SHE GOT FAT ...!!?

HIROTAKA WAKAMATSU'S REACTION

ALMOST FORGOT.
HERE, WAKA.
HAND-MADE BY LORELAI!
HUH?
OH!
THANK YOU VERY MUCH!
ばっ
BA (FWOOSH)

もぐ
MOGU (MUNCH)
OH.
THEY'RE GOOD...
HMM?
THERE'S SOMETHING WRITTEN ON THIS ONE...

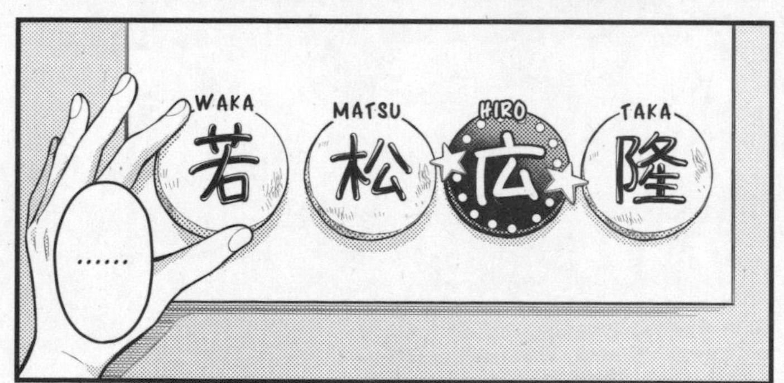
WAKA
若
MATSU
松
HIRO
広
TAKA
隆
......

SO EVER SINCE I GAVE HIM THOSE COOKIES...
...WAKA'S BEEN MAKING THIS WEIRD FACE AT ME...
?
MAYBE THEY WERE GROSS?
WHA?
MY HIRO-KUN SAID THEY WERE REALLY YUMMY!
I WONDER WHAT'S UP WITH HIM.

COOKIE RANKING

HAH!
WAIT A MINUTE ...
LOOK ...!!!
!
PINE, BAMBOO, AND PLUM!
ALL TOGETHER!!!
松
PINE
竹
BAMBOO
梅
PLUM
PINE'S S'POSED TO BE THE BEST, BUT LOOK HOW SIMPLE IT IS!!!
AND LOOK AT HOW GAUDY THE LOWLY PLUM IS!!!

TRANSLATION NOTES

PAGE 98
Escabeche is the name for a number of Latin dishes consisting of fish, meat, or vegetables cooked in vinegar and colored with paprika, and **Amatriciana** is a traditional Italian pasta sauce.

PAGE 114
Burdock root and ***shiitake*** **mushrooms** are frequently used in Japanese cooking. Burdock resembles a tree root or stick, so it isn't usually confused with *shiitake* mushrooms (which look like typical mushrooms).

PAGE 138
Japanese names are written with Chinese characters known as ***kanji***. They can be read in several different ways, or can be written phonetically using one of the two other scripts commonly used in Japanese writing. Kanji are more difficult to write because of the number of strokes, hence the comment "**Why are they all kanji...?**" comment.

PAGE 143
One of the *kanji* in Nozaki's name is also used in the Japanese word for "**fat**."

PAGE 144
The dark-colored cookie with stars can be pronounced "**hiro**," just like in Wakamatsu's first name. However, it is actually spelled with a different kanji, which is the reason for his strange reaction.

PAGE 145
Pine, **bamboo**, and **plum** are sometimes used as part of a quality-rating system in Japan. Plum products are considered the cheapest or lowest quality, while pine is used to designate more expensive or better-quality products.

PAGE 164
-Shi is a more formal version of -san that is common to written Japanese. It is the default honorific used in newspapers.

PAGE 167
Toyotomi **Hideyoshi** is a famous political figure in Japanese history, primarily because he was one of the leading figures in the unification of Japan in the sixteenth century.

PAGE 173
The Japanese term for the type of games the two are playing is "*gyaru games*," which are usually dating sims that are on the more erotic side, aimed specifically at men. **"Dating sims"** was used since female-oriented dating sim games are more commonly called "***otome***" or "reverse harem games" in English.

ink

UM...
YOUR NAME IS...?
MY NAME IS HORI.
WH—
WHAT DO YOU LIKE TO DO...?
KACHA (CLINK)
カチャッ
I DABBLE IN ACTING.
WH—
WHAT DO YOU LOOK FOR IN A WOMAN...?
...
HMMM ...
I'M A BIT EMBARRASSED TO SAY, BUT...
...BEAUTIFUL LEGS...
I WON'T ALLOW YOU TO LEAVE, NO MATTER WHAT WEIRD THINGS YOU SAY.
[ISSUE 127]

WIDE, BUT ALSO NARROW

HUUUH!!?
A TEA PARTY WITH YOUR SISTER!!?

TECHNICALLY ALSO WITH MY SISTER'S FRIEND...
...BUT YES.
FRIEND
FRIEND
SISTER
BOTH OF THEM.
C'MON.
THAT MAKES IT SOUND EVEN MORE ABSURD!!!
WHY ARE YOU TALKING TO ME ABOUT THIS!!?

I'M SUPPOSED TO INTRODUCE THEM TO A MAN.
LOOKING FOR A MAN
THAT'S A PRETTY WIDE NET.

THINK ABOUT IT.
THE ONLY PERSON I COULD POSSIBLY BRING TO MEET THEM IS YOU, HORI-SENPAI.
LOOKING FOR MASAYUKI HORI
WAIT... IS IT WIDE-OPEN OR SUPER-NARROW? TELL ME!
WHAT SHOULD I EXPECT HERE?

A BOTHERSOME GIRL

WELL, THE PROBLEM IS MY SISTER'S FRIEND ISN'T USED TO BEING OUT IN THE REAL WORLD...
YOU MAKE IT SOUND LIKE YOUR SISTER IS USED TO BEING OUT IN THE REAL WORLD.
SHE'S PRETTY BAD HERSELF.
THEY SURELY MUST BE DATING!!!

OH, THERE!!!
THAT'S HER.
WHATCHA DOING?
HEY, THERE'S A GUY WITH HER.
HE HITTING ON HER?

YOU'RE CUTE.
YOU WANNA GET OUTTA HERE WITH ME?
OH.
I KNOW WHERE THIS IS HEADED...
OW, STOP!
EEEEK, STOP!
YOU PIG!!!
GIRLS LIKE THIS...

UM...
ARE YOU...
...ASKING ME ON A DATE!?
ARE YOU CON-FESSING YOUR LOVE!?
ARE YOU IN LOVE WITH ME!?
I WAS TOTALLY WRONG, BUT THIS IS STILL GONNA BE ROUGH!!!

ROLLER COASTER

P—
PLEASED TO MEET YOU.
GATA (TREMBLE)
I'M YOSHINO, REI-SAN'S FRIEND.
GATA
GATA

IT'S ALL RIGHT. JUST RELAX A LITTLE.
EEK!
I'M SO SOR—
GASHAN (CLATTER)
AAAAAAH!

EXCUSE ME, MISS.
SU (FWISH)
HERE. I BROUGHT YOU A NEW FORK.
AAAAAAH!!

IT'S LOVE...
TOKUN (BATHUMP)
SERIOUSLY, SETTLE DOWN.

HER FAVORITE BOOK

YOSHINO-SAN IS SO UNUSED TO BEING AROUND MEN...
...THAT IT'S ENOUGH TO MAKE EVEN ME WORRY ABOUT HER...
IT MUST BE PRETTY BAD TO MAKE YOUR SISTER GET THAT SERIOUS.

WAIT.
YOU'RE NOT MAKING A HUGE FUSS LIKE YOU DID BEFORE...
"THEY MUST BE A COUPLE!!" AND ALL THAT...
HORI-SAMA.
YOU MAY NOT REALIZE IT, BUT I LEARNED EVERYTHING I KNOW FROM SHOUJO MANGA.

IF WE WERE TO PUT YOSHINO-SAN'S ACTIONS INTO A MANGA, IT WOULD END UP LIKE THIS!!
BWEH-HEH-HEH... FOUND ME A CUTE ONE!
EEK!
DOKI (BADMP) ドキドキ DOKI
H-HE HUGGED ME...
COULD IT BE THAT HE LOVES ME...?
HEY!
GET BACK HERE!!!
!!!
HE'S RUNNING AFTER ME...!!?
DOKI ドキドキ DOKI
COULD HE BE IN LOVE WITH ME...!!?
IT'S SIMPLY ABSURD!!!

BOOK: LET'S FALL IN LOVE ♡

NO, IT'S NOT.
THAT STUFF WOULD TOTALLY HAPPEN IN A SAKIKO YUMENO MANGA!!!
恋しよっ♡
ROMANCE COMIC
HE'D DO THAT...!!!
DON'T MOCK YUMENO-SENSEI!!!

A BOTHERSOME PERSON

SO I'M HERE TO TRY TO GET HER USED TO BEING AROUND GUYS...?

I-I-I-I—

I'M GRATEFUL FOR YOUR HELP!

THIS REQUEST IS EVEN WORSE THAN I THOUGHT...

... WAIT.
YOU'RE OKAY WITH KASHIMA?
SHE DOESN'T MAKE YOUR HEART POUND?
YUU-SAMA IS VERY HANDSOME, BUT SHE'S STILL A WOMAN...
I LOOK UP TO HER...

HUH.
OKAY...
KOKU (NOD)
KOKU
......

...BUT JUST LOOK AT THAT FACE!
WOMAN OR NOT— IT'S GOTTA GET TO YOU.
C'MON— REEEALLY LOOK AT HER.
HORI-SAMA, THAT DOESN'T MATTER RIGHT NOW.

AS THE PRESIDENT OF THE DRAMA CLUB

YOU'RE EXTRA SERIOUS TODAY, LITTLE KASHIMA...

YES...

SHE'S LIKELY TO FOLLOW SOME STRANGE MAN WHEN NO ONE IS WATCHING.

THAT IS HARDLY FUNNY.

WHAT I WANT YOU TO DO...
...IS TURN ON ALL YOUR CHARM AND TRY TO SEDUCE HER.
SO WE CAN BUILD UP HER RESISTANCE...
OH... I GET IT...
SO THAT'S WHY YOU WANTED ME HERE?
I AM AN ACTOR, AFTER ALL.

IN THAT CASE, MIGHT AS WELL PLAY ALONG...
A GUY WHO MAKES HER GO WEAK AT THE KNEES...
I CAN DO THAT!!!

YOU'VE BEEN STARING AT ME ...!!!
WHAT DO I DO?
MY HEART'S BEATING WILDLY!!!
DAM-MIT!
THERE'S NO CHAL-LENGE TO THIS!!!

NO MATTER WHAT HE SAYS

GUESS WHAT? I'M ACTUALLY PRETTY GOOD AT READING PALMS.
YOU CAN READ PALMS? THAT'S SIMPLY SPLENDID!!!

CAN I READ YOUR PALM?
Y— YOU WANT TO LOOK AT MY HAND!!?
IT'S BEATING EVEN FASTER!!!

JUST KIDDING!
KYU (SQUEEZE)
I JUST WANTED TO HOLD YOUR HAND.
HWAAAAH! YOU'RE SO COOOOOOL ~~!!!
A PRINCE ...!!! YOU'RE LIKE A PRINCE ~~!!!
AAAAAAH!

......
WERE YOU DROPPED ON YOUR HEAD AS A CHILD ...?
Y-YOU'RE WORRIED ABOUT ME!!?
SO KIND —
GEHO (COUGH)
GEHO GEHO
げほげほげほ

A STRAY BULLET

HORI-SENPAI.
Your acting!!
YOU'RE SLIPPING OUT OF THE ROLE!
Y— YEAH.
GUESS I WAS...
PICK-UP LINES, HUH...?

...IS THIS THE FIRST TIME WE'VE MET?
'COS I FEEL LIKE I'VE LOVED YOU FOR FOREVER.
ドキッ
DOKI (BADMP)
!!!

I LOVE YOUR KIND EYES.
AND I WANT...
...YOUR CUTE VOICE ALL TO MY-SELF.
きゅんっ
KYUN (TWINGE)
AAAAAH!!
AAAAH!

?
WHY IS REI REACTING THE SAME WAY...?
THAT'S THE LINE SUZUKI-KUN WHISPERED TO THE DOLPHIN...
...IN THE FIRST CHAPTER OF LET'S FALL IN LOVE ♡!!!
はわわわ
HAWAWAWA (PANIC)
I LOVE YOUR KIND EYES. ♡
OH, SUZUKI-KUN...

SAY NO ①

MAYBE INSTEAD OF BUILDING UP HER RESISTANCE, WE SHOULD FOCUS ON GETTING HER TO TURN DOWN GUYS...
OH.
YEAH, YOU'RE RIGHT.
OKAY, YOSHINO-SAN.
NO MATTER WHAT HORI-SENPAI SAYS, JUST SAY NO, OKAY?
YES!

HEY, THIS PLACE IS NICE AND ALL...
...BUT DO YOU WANNA HAVE SOME COFFEE AT MY PLACE?
EEK!
YOU'RE INVITING ME TO YOUR PLACE, SO THAT MEANS YOUR INTENTIONS ARE SERIOUS...!!!
I'D LOVE TO GO!!!

......
SO YOU KNOW, NO ONE ELSE IS THERE RIGHT NOW.
YOU'RE SAYING THERE'S NO NEED TO WORRY ABOUT MY BEHAVIOR? HOW KIND!!
I'D LOVE TO GO!!!

...TO BE HONEST, MY PET SNAKES GOT OUT THIS MORNING...
...AND THEY'RE SOMEWHERE IN THE HOUSE.
THERE ARE TWO...
...NO, FIVE OF THEM...
SENPAI!!!
YOU TURNED IT INTO A GAME TO SEE WHAT IT TAKES TO MAKE HER SAY NO!!!
COME BACK TO US!!!

TURN HIM DOWN NORMALLY

YOU SAID I SHOULD SAY NO...
...BUT HOW AM I SUPPOSED TO TURN HIM DOWN ...?
JUST DO IT. ACT NORMAL.
HEY.
YOU WANNA COME TO MY PLACE FOR COFFEE?

DRINK COFFEE?
WITH YOU?
I'M SURE YOU USE FRESH BEANS TO MAKE IT FROM SCRATCH ...
...BUT I HARDLY THINK YOU CAN MATCH MY COFFEE...
WHY DID YOU ESCALATE IT...?

SO?
WHAT BEANS DO YOU USE?
SINCE YOU'RE ASKING ME TO TRY IT...
...YOU MUST HAVE A FAVORITE VARIETY, RIGHT?
SHE'S STARTING TO SOUND LIKE A REAL JERK. IT'S ACTUALLY PRETTY IMPRES-SIVE...

BUT SINCE YOU'D BE THE ONE MAKING IT...
...I'D BE FINE WITH INSTANT COFFEE.
NIKO (SMILE)
KYUN (TWINGE)
KASHIMA ...!!!
WHY ARE YOU SEDUCING HIM BACK, ONEE-SAMA?
COME BACK TO US!

SAY NO ②

OKAY.
ALL YOU HAVE TO SAY IS, "I'M SORRY. I'M A BIT BUSY RIGHT NOW..."
Oh!
That's a simple phrase to use when someone tries to pick you up.
I SHALL DO MY BEST!!

HEY!
YOU'RE PRETTY CUTE.
WANNA GO HAVE A GOOD TIME?
I—
I'M SORRY. I'M BUSY RIGHT NOW...
OHHHH!!

YOU DID IT!!
I TURNED HIM DOWN!!!
AMAZING!
OKAY.
YOU CAN USE THAT WHEN THEY DON'T LET YOU GO TOO.
SO WHAT'RE YOU SO BUSY DOING?

U—
Umm ...
I'm busy watching you.
DON'T TURN IT INTO A YES!

HE'S NEVER HAD THAT REACTION BEFORE

HUH...? WAIT A MINUTE.
YOU'VE BEEN TALKING TO HORI-SENPAI FOR A PRETTY LONG TIME NOW, HAVEN'T YOU...?
HAH!
!!!
!!

OH MY!!! PERHAPS THAT MEANS SHE'S BUILT UP A BIT OF TOLERANCE !!
NOW THAT YOU MENTION IT...
...I'M ABLE TO TALK WITHOUT STARING QUITE SO MUCH!!
GOOD FOR YOU!!!
OHHHHHH!
THAT GROUP OVER THERE...

Heeeey, Kashima.
Whatcha doing with these sweet things?
Hello, ladies! Would you like to spend some time with me...
...my sweet, little kittens? ♡

JUST KID—
GATA (CLATTER)
DAMMIT, MIKO-SHIBA!!!
GATA
GATA

IT'S TOO EMBARRASSING!!!

OH... I GET IT...SO SHE'S GOT ISSUES...
SORRY FOR COMING IN AT THE WORST TIME...
NOT ONLY DOES SHE GET CARRIED AWAY WAY TOO EASILY, SHE ALSO HAS THE WORST TASTE IN MEN.
I'M WORRIED ABOUT HER...
WHAA...?
DID SHE GO OFF WITH A SUPER-SKETCHY GUY EARLIER?

....
SURE, KASHIMA'S A GIRL...BUT YOSHINO STILL SHOULD'VE CHOSEN KASHIMA FIRST...!
HMPH!
YOU... ...KA-SHIMA FANBOY ...!!!

Y'KNOW... ...I THOUGHT YOU'D CALL NOZAKI IN FOR STUFF LIKE THIS.
LEAVE IT TO ME!!
AREN'T YOU HIS FAN?
I ASKED MY SISTER TO HELP INSTEAD.
HMM?
WHAT'D YOU SAY TO HER?
I ASKED HER TO INTRODUCE SOMEONE APPROPRIATE.

"I'D LIKE YOU TO FIND THE MOST WONDERFUL MAN...
"...YOU KNOW."
BY THE WAY, WHAT ARE THEY TO EACH OTHER!!?

特別BLOG
SPECIAL

Whaaaa~!?☆ 00/00/00

PLEASE!!
[ISSUE 128]

Oh no...Can I really do this...?
But my editor, K-san, asked me to do it...so I'll give it my best shot!!
Goooo me! ☆

THE ONLY ANSWER IS YES

YUMENO-SENSEI. DO YOU HAVE A WEEK FREE TO WORK ON SOMETHING ...?
!!!
'COS YOU WANT TO TAKE ME ON A RESEARCH TRIP ...!!?
No.

ACTUALLY, FOR THE TWENTY-FIFTH ANNIVERSARY OF *GIRLS' ROMANCE* ...
...WE'RE HAVING VARIOUS ARTISTS TAKE OVER THE BLOG...
FOR A WEEK AT A-TIME...
The blog ...?

IF HE CAN'T...
...I'LL DO IT FOR HIM!!
AS YUMENO-SENSEI!!

THIS IS PRETTY IMPRESSIVE.
YOU GOT EVERY ONE OF THEM TO AGREE RIGHT AWAY.
OHH?
GUESS THEY ALL JUST WANNA STAND OUT!
THEY WERE TOTALLY ON BOARD!!

THE BLOG OF A MANGA CREATOR

...SO...
...I'LL BE BLOGGING ABOUT SAKIKO YUMENO'S DAILY LIFE.

ANY THOUGHTS ON WHAT TYPES OF EVENTS WILL GO OVER BEST WITH READERS ...!?
I HAVE SEVEN DAYS TO FILL!!!
HE NEVER HAD ANY INTENTION OF TALKING ABOUT HIS ACTUAL DAILY LIFE...!!!

UMM... WELL...
WHAT IF YOU GIVE PEOPLE A SNEAK PEEK AT THE MANGA YOU'RE WORKING ON RIGHT NOW?
IT MIGHT BE FUN TO TALK ABOUT WHAT GOES INTO MAKING MANGA TOO!
I had to redo this shot of Mamiko three times! ✩
MY CURRENT PROJECT, HUH...?

DON'T YOU THINK PEOPLE WILL JUST GET ANNOYED? LIKE, "YOU'RE ALWAYS TALKING ABOUT MANGA, EVEN NOW!!"
SHEESH—SHE THINKS SHE'S SO HIGH AND MIGHTY!
PE (PTOOEY)
WHAT EXACTLY D'YOU THINK READERS WANT FROM YOU ANYWAY?

THE REFERENCE

WHY DON'T YOU TAKE A LOOK AT THE PERSON WHO DID THE LAST SET OF BLOG ENTRIES TO SEE WHAT THEY DID?
KACHI (CLICK)
KACHI
THE GIRLS' ROMANCE SPECIAL BLOG...
OH YEAH.

Nice to meet you!!
Hello! I'm Nikki-sensei, and I'm going to be taking over the blog for a bit.
I'll be here for the next week!!
WHA!?
SHE'S SHOWING HER FACE!!?
I MEAN, SHE'S GOT A MASK ON, BUT WHY SHOW HERSELF AT ALL!!?
ISN'T SHE A MANGA CREATOR!!?

I'm stuck on my next rough draft, so I decided to cook something! Oh, whoops! I guess this is my manga~! ☆
WHAT'S WRONG WITH HER!!?
SHE'S GONE FULL STAND-UP!!!
THIS WON'T HELP US!!!

I just can't help but think of poetry late at night.
Twinkle, twinkle, little star. ♡
My heart's all full of clouds. ☆
My editor, M-shi, should become a star. ♡♡
DON'T TELL ME SHE USED MAENO'S BLOG AS HER REFERENCE...?

BLOG IDEAS

WAIT A SEC!
WHY IS EVERYONE HERE SO USELESS WHEN IT COMES TO SOCIAL MEDIA!!?
STUPID GIRLS' ROMANCE!!!
IF WE GO ON SOCIAL MEDIA, WE HAVE TO DEAL WITH MAENO-SAN...
HE'S GOT WAY TOO MUCH CLOUT!!!

NEVER MIND HIM.
I NEED TO WORK ON MY IDEAS FOR THE BLOG...
I'M PRETTY SURE THIS IS THE LAYOUT...
BLOG
TITLE
ENTRY
YOU'RE DOING IT ANALOG!!?

I'LL START BY HAVING THE FIRST DAY BE SOMETHING LIKE THIS...

HELLO, IT'S YUM ENOUGH AWWW~! I MESSED UP~ STUPID AUTOCORRECT~!!

THIS IS MORE THAN JUST NOT BEING GREAT WITH SOCIAL MEDIA!!!

AND THEN, HERE'S THE SEVENTH AND FINAL DAY.

I'VE MASTERED TOUCH-TYPING.

IS SHE REPORTING ON HER PROGRESS IN A COMPUTER CLASS!?

BOTH OF THEM

ARE YOU REALLY SURE ABOUT JUST PUTTING UP SELF-PORTRAITS ON THE BLOG?
SHE MIGHT BE TOO CUTE!
WHA!!? DON'T THE READERS WANNA KNOW ABOUT ME!?

WHAT DO YOU THINK, SAKURA!!?
HUH...!!?
OF COURSE I WANNA KNOW ABOUT YOU!!!
SO I'M SURE EVERYONE ELSE DOES TOO!!!

LIKE WHAT YOU WEAR WHEN YOU'RE LOUNGING AROUND THE HOUSE.
OR WHAT YOU DRINK RIGHT AFTER YOU GET OUT OF THE BATH.
STOP LYING!!!

...A WHITE CAMI-SOLE...
...WITH PINK SHORTS.
AND AFTER TAKING A BATH, BUBBLE-TEA—
STOP LYING!!!

A GENTLER RESPONSE

OH, I KNOW.
THIS MANGA CREATOR'S AFTERWORDS ARE REALLY POPULAR.
THEY'RE TRUE STORIES.
OH?
LIKE WHAT?

IT'S MOSTLY ABOUT HER YOUNGER BROTHER. HE'S REALLY FUN TO WATCH.
NEE-CHAN...
I THINK I CAME UP WITH A SHOUJO MANGA...
MY LITTLE BROTHER
FOR REAL?
THAT'S GREAT!
THIS IS THE HEROINE'S BEST FRIEND...
A THIRD EYE
HIDEYOSHI REINCARNATED
THAT'S A LOT GOING ON ALL AT ONCE!!!
OHH... THAT'S A GOOD IDEA.

DON'T FOCUS ON THE ARTIST (FEMALE), BUT ON THE BROTHER!!! MEANING THE OPPOSITE SEX GOES OVER BETTER WITH READERS!!!
THAT'S THE MESSAGE HERE!!!
UM...NO, IT'S ABOUT WHAT HAPPENS...
IT JUST SO HAPPENS I HAVE A LITTLE BROTHER OF MY OWN!!!
SO NOW, THEY'LL GO EASIER ON ME TOO!!!
HA-HA-HA-HA-HA!

BA (BAM)
WELL!!?
MY LITTLE BROTHER
LAST WEEK
THE DAY BEFORE YESTERDAY
YESTERDAY
U-UMMM!
I LIKE THAT YOU DIDN'T COPY IT BUT DREW A NEW PICTURE EVERY TIME!!
GOOD ONE, NOZAKI-KUN!!!

DRAMATIZATION

YOU CAN'T PUT HIM IN AS IS. THAT'S BORING.
WHY DON'T YOU DRAMATIZE IT? MAKE IT A BIT OVER-THE-TOP...?
HMM ...
I'M NOT REALLY A FAN OF THAT SORT OF THING...

MAYU.
MAYU, WAKE UP.
WANT SOME SNACKS?
WHAT D'YOU WANNA EAT?
......
RICE BALLS ...

MY LITTLE BROTHER JUST LOVES MY COOKING! ♡
I WANNA EAT YOUR RICE BALLS, ONEE-CHAN...
HE COMES TO VISIT ME AT WORK EVERY DAY. ☆
LOOKS GOOD!

BUT HE'S ACTUALLY REALLY POPULAR AT SCHOOL!!!
ALL THE GIRLS ARE CRAZY ABOUT HIM. IT'S LIKE HE'S A TOTALLY DIFFERENT PERSON... (LOL)
EEEP!!
EEEP!!
EEEP!!
THAT'S A DIFFERENT PERSON.

TRUTH IS STRANGER...

YOU CAN'T MAKE EVERY SINGLE THING UP, YOU KNOW!
HEY, MAYU.
YOU BEEN CHANGING IT UP LATELY?
LATELY ...?

I'VE BEEN ...
... TAKING PICS WITH MY PHONE.
PASHA (SNAP)
OH!
I GUESS I HAVE SEEN YOU DOING THAT.

AND THEN I SHOW THEM TO THE GIRLS AT SCHOOL.
KASHA
WHA !!?
WAIT... IS THIS ...!!?
I FOUND A PRETTY FLOWER.
OOH!
THAT'S JUST ADORABLE!!

KASHA
NOZAKI.
I COVERED FOR YOU WHEN YOU WERE NAPPING AGAIN.
PAY UP.
SU (FWISH)
AAAAH, HE'S SO HOT !!!
IT'S A NEW ONE !!!
EEEEEEP!
SO COOL!!!

CAN'T SAY ANY MORE

OH REALLY? MY LITTLE MAYU?
SO ARE THERE ANY GIRLS IN THAT GROUP WHO YOU HAVE YOUR EYE ON?
WHO I HAVE MY EYE ON...?

HUH? MY BROTHER?
YEAH, HE DOES JUDO AT HIS SCHOOL.
THERE IS ONE.

REALLY!!? WHAT'S SHE LIKE —!!?
HER BROTHER IS ON THE JUDO TEAM...
OHHH!!?
AND!? WHAT ELSE!!?

I CAN'T REALLY SAY ANY MORE...
HEY, YOU BARELY GAVE ME A THING!

GIRLS' ROMANCE READERS

ALSO, SHE LIKES HOW YOU LOOK, MIKOTO-SAN...
?
WHY ME?
I THINK I CAN WORK WITH THAT.
?
WHAT DO YOU MEAN?

LOOK, LIKE THIS...
I THINK MY LITTLE BROTHER IS IN LOVE. ♡
AWA あわ あわ AWA (PANIC)
WHO IS IT!?
WHAT'S SHE LIKE?
ME
MY ASSISTANT M-KUN
OHHH!!
LITTLE BROTHER AND LOVE!!!

HAH!
WAIT, STOP!!! NOZAKI-KUN!!!
ARE YOU USING "MY ASSISTANT M-KUN"—!?
YUMENO-SENSEI IS S'POSED TO BE A HIGH SCHOOL GIRL!!!
!!
YOU'RE RIGHT!! I DON'T WANT TO GIVE ANYONE ANY STRANGE IDEAS!!!
I'LL CHANGE IT TO "M-CHAN"!!!

LATER, ON THE BLOG
MY ASSISTANT M-CHAN
I wonder if he likes a girl from his class...?
Comments
· It's definitely M-chan!
· He totally likes M-chan, right...?
· Sensei, don't you see it!?

AAAAH!
THEY GOT THE WRONG IDEA FOR SURE!!!

CHIYO-CHAN'S STAND-IN

NOZAKI-KUN... ...I WANT IN TOO.
HUH!!?
YOU WANT TO BE IN IT!!?

NO, I CAN'T. IF I PUT SAKURA IN AS WELL, IT'LL TURN INTO A LOVE TRIANGLE!!!
I DON'T WANT SAKIKO YUMENO'S WORKPLACE TURNING INTO A DRAMA PIT!!!
C-→ CHAN
Comments
· Who is that girl...!!?
· A new challenger!!
· Your brother's super-popular. (lol)

I KNOW!!!
I'LL DO THIS...!!!
C-CHAN, WANT SOME CANDY?
OKAY!
NO...!!! SURE, THIS WILL PREVENT MORE ROMANTIC TANGLES...
...BUT THERE'S NO WAY SAKURA WON'T HATE IT...!!!

ぱっ
BA (FWOOSH)
YOU'RE FINE WITH THIS!!?

SAKURA'S FOCUS

I'M SO CLOSE TO NOZAKI-KUN!!!
H— HE'S HUGGING ME!!!
RAN (INTENSE) らん
RAN らん
RAN らん
I GUESS...
...SHE'S NOT THAT WORRIED ABOUT HOW SHE LOOKS.
THAT HELPS.

OKAY, THEN...
...LET'S MAKE IT OBVIOUS THAT M-CHAN AND MY BROTHER REALLY ARE JUST FRIENDS.
TOTAL FOCUS...
...ON THE GAME.
HONESTLY! THEY'RE BOTH OBSESSED WITH DATING SIMS!
GET TO WORK.

UM... NOZAKI-KUN...
ABOUT C-CHAN...
SHE'S SITTING ON YOUR HAND...
!!!
BIKU (FLINCH) びくっ
SO SHE REALLY ISN'T OKAY WITH IT AFTER ALL!!?

WHEN YOU'RE HOLDING C-CHAN, IT SHOULD BE MORE, YOU KNOW...
LIKE YOU'RE HOLDING HER TIGHT, WITH BOTH HANDS...
KYU (SQUEEZE) きゅっ
KYU きゅっ
JUST THE HOLD—!!?

THE LOSERS

WHOA, DID HE REALLY RUN WITH THE LITTLE BROTHER THING THE ENTIRE WEEK...?
HE EVEN THREW ME IN THERE...
FURU (SHAKE) FURU
ふるふる
NO.
HUH?

My little brother watches quietly while I work.

Comments

- So cute.
- So cute!!!
- Your brother's so cuuute~! ♡

GEEZ!!
WE KNOW YOU'RE THERE!
AH HA HA!
COME ON IN.

C-chan just loves cheesecake.

Comments

- So cuuuuute!!!
- Too cute!!!
- So cute!!!

MORI (CHOMP) MORI
もりもり

TO-DAY'S C-CHAN
I WANT SOME YUMMY CHOC-OLATE!
I gave her some chocolate cake.
Comments
· So cuuute!!!
· I wanna give her chocolate!!!
· More C-chan...!!!
WE GOT REPLACED.
BY CHIYO-SAN.
THAT DUMPLING IS STRONG ...

THE REAL IMAGE

OHHH.
SO M IS MIKO-SHIBA?
REALLY? I THOUGHT YOUR LITTLE BRO GOT HIMSELF A GIRLFRIEND.

IF I WERE TO DRAW IT FOR REAL, IT'D BE SOMETHING LIKE THIS.
OH. YOU UP?
WANT SOME-THING TO DRINK?
HEH! IT'S A BUNCH OF GUYS.
NOT SEXY AT ALL.

OH... SO THAT DUMPLING YOU'RE ALWAYS HOLDING...
...IS SAKURA ...?
GASHI (RUB)
GASHI
HA-HA-HA.
YEAH, IT IS.
IF I WERE TO DRAW IT FOR REAL ...

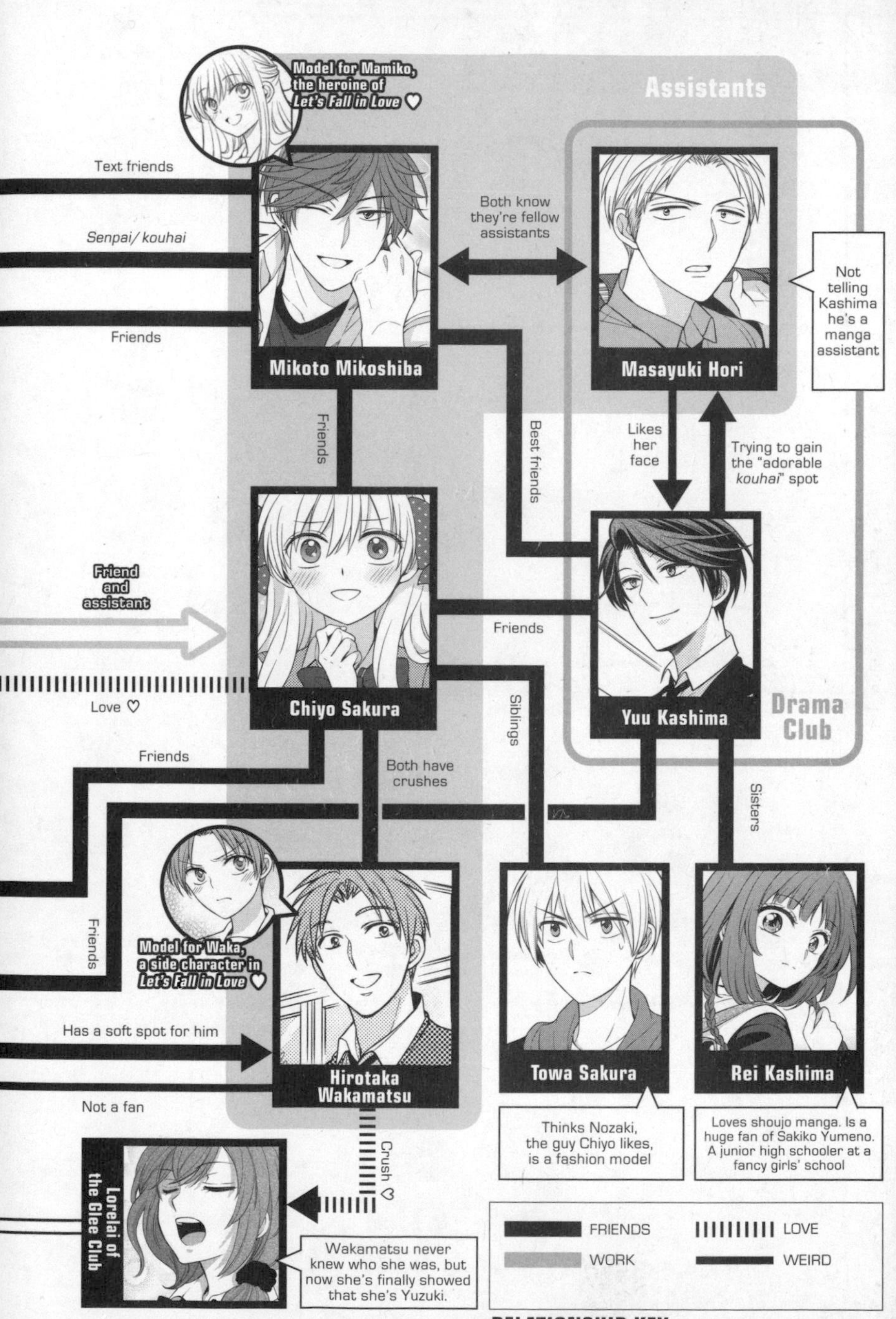
Model for Mamiko, the heroine of *Let's Fall in Love* ♡
Assistants
Text friends
Senpai/ kouhai
Friends
Mikoto Mikoshiba
Both know they're fellow assistants
Masayuki Hori
Not telling Kashima he's a manga assistant
Friends
Best friends
Likes her face
Trying to gain the "adorable *kouhai*" spot
Friend and assistant
Chiyo Sakura
Friends
Yuu Kashima
Love ♡
Siblings
Drama Club
Friends
Both have crushes
Sisters
Friends
Model for Waka, a side character in *Let's Fall in Love* ♡
Has a soft spot for him
Hirotaka Wakamatsu
Towa Sakura
Rei Kashima
Not a fan
Thinks Nozaki, the guy Chiyo likes, is a fashion model
Loves shoujo manga. Is a huge fan of Sakiko Yumeno. A junior high schooler at a fancy girls' school
Crush ♡
Lorelai of the Glee Club
Wakamatsu never knew who she was, but now she's finally showed that she's Yuzuki.
FRIENDS
LOVE
WORK
WEIRD
RELATIONSHIP KEY

Relationship Chart
SECRET
Mayu-Mayu
Same person
The youngest child of the Nozaki family and the source of Nozaki's pen name
Yumeko Nozaki
Mayu Nozaki
Brothers
Monthly Girls' Romance Editorial Department
Friends!
Coworkers
Annoying
Mitsuya Maeno
Ken Miyamae
Thinks Ken-san is cool
Editor
Traumatized
Former editor
Umetarou Nozaki
Editor
Not a fan
Manga-ka friends
Friends
Siblings
Yukari Miyako
Has a crush, but she has no clue
Ryousuke Seo
Yuzuki Seo
Has pity for Wakamatsu, the guy his sister took a liking to
Model for Oze, a side character in Let's Fall in Love ♡
Same person
A RELATIONSHIP CHART FOR THE MOST OBVIOUS THINGS AS OF THE END OF VOLUME 13!

MONTHLY GIRLS' NOZA

Izumi Ts

Translation: Leighann Harvey
Lettering: Lys Blakeslee

Yen Press
150 West 30th Street, 19th Floor
New York, NY 10001

Visit us!
yenpress.com
facebook.com/yenpress
twitter.com/yenpress
yenpress.tumblr.com
instagram.com/yenpress

First Yen Press Print Edition: June 2022
Edited by Yen Press Editorial: Danielle Niederkorn
Designed by Yen Press Design: Wendy Chan

Library of Congress Control Number: 2015952610

ISBN: 978-1-9753-4723-9 (paperback)
978-1-9753-4724-6 (ebook)

10 9 8 7 6 5 4 3 2 1

WOR

Printed in the United States of America